HELP!
I'm a Dad

**All a new dad needs to know about
the difficult first few months**

Nick Harper

Michael O'Mara Books Limited

First published in Great Britain in 2014 by
Michael O'Mara Books Limited
9 Lion Yard
Tremadoc Road
London SW4 7NQ

A CIP catalogue record for this book is available from the British Library.

Papers used by Michael O'Mara Books Limited are natural, recyclable products made from wood grown in sustainable forests. The manufacturing processes conform to the environmental regulations of the country of origin.

ISBN: 978-1-78243-224-1 in paperback print format
ISBN: 978-1-78243-238-8 in ebook format

1 2 3 4 5 6 7 8 9 10

Designed and typeset by K DESIGN, Winscombe, Somerset
Cover design by Ana Bježančević
Illustrations by David Woodroffe and from www.shutterstock.com

Printed and bound by CPI Group (UK) Ltd, Croydon, CR0 4YY

www.mombooks.com

CONTENTS

Dedication

This book wouldn't have been written
without the help of …

Mr A. Gudi and staff at the Fertility Centre,
Homerton University Hospital,
London.

The staff at SCBU,
Whipps Cross University Hospital,
London.

And most of all my wife
Sarah Harper,
the amazing mum of Louis and James.

INTRODUCTION

WELCOME
TO THE CLUB

Hello and welcome.
And of course, huge congratulations.

If you are reading these words, it's because you are about to – or indeed have – become a dad for the first time. For that you should feel very proud. Mildly terrified too, but very proud.

As a new dad, your life is about to change in so many ways – and almost all of them for the better. Your baby will suddenly bring new meaning, purpose and direction to your life. You will feel a very rare brand of love that your heart reserves only for your baby and suddenly, for the first time, the world and your place in it will all begin to make sense. Although probably not straight away.

At first you won't have a clue what you're supposed to be doing, because being a dad for the very first time is a confusing, complicated business with a very, very steep learning curve.

For example, you won't know how to make your baby stop crying, or what clothes a newborn baby should be wearing, or how, what and when to feed him or her. You won't know if fifty-three nappy changes in a single afternoon is more or less than normal, or where your baby should sleep, or when, or for how long. And unless you're a qualified doctor or midwife, you probably won't know if that throaty little cough you hear in the dead of night is the first strain of some life-threatening illness that needs urgent medical attention, or just a throaty little cough.

Initially, you won't know very much at all. But don't worry. That's normal and you're not alone.

Apparently, 255 babies are born around the world every single minute – 4.3 every second of every day. Most of those babies are born to parents who haven't got a clue what they're meant to be doing. Not because they're bad parents, but because nobody really knows what they're doing when they become a dad (or a mum) for the first time.

Some people might pretend they know. Some people might even make a career out of their supposed expertise, and some charlatans may even, ahem, write books on the subject, as if they somehow hold the secret to it all. But they don't. Because how could they?

Every newborn baby is unique and no single set of rules can ever cover every issue that will crop up in the first year. What works for one baby won't necessarily work for another and much of the first year will involve trial and error on your part, mixed in with a lot of guesswork. This is normal.

I remember how I felt when I first became a dad. Confused and terrified. But mainly confused. My wife and I had been handed our babies (plural, two, twins) and been told to go home and, like everyone else has done before us, just get on with it. The hospital staff were magnificent and more polite than that, but that was the gist of it – we were taking up a bed another mother needed and they were busy, so it was time we left.

We did so very nervously, took an hour to drive the ten minutes home, travelling at snail's pace and avoiding all the speed bumps, and finally reached our front door. And as we closed it with a terrifying click behind us, we realized that This Is How It Begins – the responsibility from here on in is all ours. We looked at each other and asked the same question: 'So what are we supposed to do now?' Neither of us really knew.

We'd been through numerous Preparing Parents For Baby courses in the weeks leading up to that day, each designed to teach us exactly what to do when our babies arrived. But none of them can really ready you for that moment when you are staring down at a tiny little baby whose life is entirely dependent on you and your partner. It's the strangest feeling of ecstatic terror you will ever encounter.

Not knowing what to do with a *real* baby, as opposed to the tatty plastic toy we passed around parent class, my wife and I decided that the best thing we could do was sit down and have a nice cup of tea and just see how things unfolded.

It's all you can do really, but this book has been written to try and help you make sense of a very confusing and often complicated situation, specifically from a new dad's perspective. Its sole aim is to help new dads understand a bit more about what's going on and what lies ahead, and to take at least some of the guesswork out of the first few weeks and months.

It's also been written to cover only the first twelve months of your baby's life, because by the time you reach Year Two you'll have a far better idea of what you're supposed to be doing.

This book doesn't claim to have all the answers to all the questions you will have as your baby slowly grows, because that would undermine what I wrote before about babies being unique individuals. It simply aims to offer as much useful advice as possible on the challenges you'll face, and by doing so, help you feel just slightly less lost and a little bit less confused.

If you are as clueless as I was when I first started out then you have a long road to travel and a lot to learn, so we should probably crack on. But why not put the kettle on first, we've got time for that.

WARNING!

As mentioned above, this is a book written by a dad, not by a doctor, nurse, midwife or health visitor. All the advice is as accurate as stringent research and tireless fact checking allows, but if in doubt about any element at any time, consult a qualified expert at the earliest opportunity. Raising a baby is a very serious business and his or her safety should never be put at risk in any way.

DADVICE   Wait For The Smile

Every parent who's been through it will tell you to 'enjoy every minute', but they'll say it from a safe distance, when their baby's bigger and life's no longer quite so confusing. The truth is you won't enjoy every minute and you shouldn't feel guilty about it.

There will be immensely long nights where you see hours that haven't existed since your partying days. There will be poo that even the strongest nappies (and clothes) cannot hold – and 'your turn' will become a very familiar cry. There will be vomit, countless meals that go cold, television programmes interrupted, nights off cancelled, friends you no longer see, a house that's no longer clean or tidy and a military-style operation every time you want to so much as pop to the supermarket.

And during those early days you will be terrified. Every cry, cough, sneeze, slight temperature, red rash, bump or mark will have you scouring the internet or calling the doctor. But then your little one smiles at you, giggles, holds your finger, sits up and calls you Daddy for the very first time and you understand how that parent could have forgotten all the other things. Enjoy every minute.

ROB J, ISABELLA AND JESSICA'S DAD

PART ONE

A CRASH COURSE IN ENTRY-LEVEL BABY BASICS

THE FIRST TWELVE MONTHS

*Before we begin in earnest, a quick guide to
what should lie ahead . . .*

So, as you drink your tea and wait for your baby to wake up and the
first visitors to arrive with their cuddly toys and hopefully some nice
champagne, you'll probably be wondering what happens next. My
guess would be that your baby will wake up and start crying, drink
some milk, do a big poo and go back to sleep again. I'm no expert but
that's as good as guaranteed.

But what then? What next? How will it all unfold?

Well, sadly, no two babies are the same so nobody can say for
sure, but there are certain milestone moments that will occur in the
first year of your baby's life and which you, the proud parent, will be
able to excitedly tick off.

Expect them to unfold something like this:

The First Month

At some point between one and four weeks, he will make eye contact and follow your face as you move in and out of focus. He may copy your grinning, gurning face but don't expect him to smile or laugh – it's not that you're not amusing, he's just not capable of doing either yet. He should be sleeping for about sixteen hours a day, including up to four naps a day – much like you used to before he arrived. (Note: I say 'he' but your baby could well be a 'she'. To cover both bases and keep all dads happy, I will use 'he' and 'she' in alternate chapters.)

The Second Month

Between four and twelve weeks, often from around six weeks, he will start smiling and laughing and generally showing more signs of recognition. Be aware though that a smiling baby often just has wind – he may not be finding your hyperactive clown routine funny in the slightest.

The Third Month

At some point between three and five months he will start to reach out and explore things, which can mean the fun stuff like his dangly toys, but also anything close to hand, like hot cups of coffee on really low tables. Make sure all the bottles of sulphuric acid are placed on high worktops, well out of reach. Your baby should also smile spontaneously and with great regularity, and start to make 'babble' noises – oohing and ahhing a lot, which in turn will make you ooh and ahh a lot.

The Fourth Month

From around now your baby will be able to roll from his front to his back – where, amusingly, he may often get stuck. This manoeuvrability is all very impressive but it does make him a danger when plonked on the bed or on a baby-changing station, so at this point you should move to a higher alert. He may well laugh out loud, and his sleeping will typically be fourteen to fifteen hours a day, with two to three daytime naps.

The Fifth Month

Between four and six months your baby may well start to eat solids. In fact, at this age he'll eat whatever he can get his hands on as he starts exploring tastes and textures of anything and everything, including carpet fluff and dirty long worms. He will also dribble more and squeal with delight.

The Sixth Month

By this point your baby will start to mimic the noises he hears, so the nursery rhymes you sing to him he can now sing back – in a fashion. He may also be capable of physically picking things up. And while there's absolutely no guarantee, for a lot of parents, sleep gets noticeably better (as in, you all get more of it) from around six months.

The Seventh Month

At some point between six and nine months, your baby may be growing his first milk teeth – teething in other words, which can lead to an increase in tears. Annoyingly, for you and your baby, his full set of first teeth can take up to twenty-four months to break through so expect some turbulence.

The Eighth Month

Your baby may be showing the first signs of sitting up without support. He will also quickly progress from sitting to crawling, or at least shuffling along on his bottom, and then on to pulling himself up and hanging on to the sideboard. And here begins a period of exploring all the dangerous corners of your house, yanking at irons and hanging off the bookcase with a smile on his face. Upgrade your alert to Code Red. He'll be sleeping less: fourteen hours a day, including a morning nap and/or afternoon siesta.

The Ninth Month

By this point your baby may have progressed from mushed and mashed food to genuine solids, some of which he'll be keen to feed himself. That said, this will be advanced but not unheard of for most babies of this age.

The Tenth Month

From around this point a really advanced baby will take his first tentative steps, wobbling uncertainly and frequently falling on his little backside with a bump and a look of confusion. Given that it takes most babies between eleven to fourteen months to take their first steps, if this happens, you should feel particularly proud.

The Eleventh Month

Your baby should have mastered a decent grip by now, which will make feeding himself finger foods much easier. He's still sleeping for fourteen hours a day, but those two daytime sleeps are getting noticeably shorter.

The Twelfth Month

By this point your baby may be able to respond to his own name and say his first words. These are usually 'Mama' and 'Dada', which is highly unoriginal but will still make your heart skip when you first hear it. By this point he is probably able to stand without support, dance badly and use a spoon, but probably not all three at the same time.

WARNING!

Competitive Parents

Please bear in mind that these stages – and when they happen – should only be used as a guide; they can naturally occur earlier or later in a child's development. If you encounter a dad or a mum who tells you their baby is sleeping through the night and eating solids at the table with a knife and fork by six weeks, try not to laugh at their ridiculous one-upmanship. All babies develop at their own pace and what they can do at six months usually has little bearing on what they achieve later in life. Don't be one of those pushy parents, and speak to a health professional if you are at all concerned.

DADVICE Just Be Grateful It Wasn't Twins (Unless Of Course It Was)

If you've got twins, you're on the frontline. You know those mornings when you're grumpy because your baby was up half the night? Well, twin dads were up half the night with one kid and then the other half with the other.

Then they become toddlers, and the trouble really starts. The bit where Junior crawls off in a random and dangerous direction? Try it when they go in opposite directions. Shall I save the one heading for the duck pond or the main road?

Their toys become weapons – one is never enough – and physical friction is never far away. It quickly becomes personal yet oddly private: they punch, then cuddle, and you're left wondering quite what to do.

But there are advantages to multiple births. You do get kudos and your hands-on role creates a genuine bond with your babies. Plus, having twins means never having to procreate again, so you'll never have to go through this all again.

GARY P, NATALIE AND ELLA'S DAD

SURVIVING THE FIRST TWENTY-FOUR HOURS

*These may well be the longest, most worrying
hours of your life . . .*

The first twenty-four hours are easily the most tricky of being a new dad and new parents, purely because you will be gripped by a fear of the unknown. As you sit there, looking at your baby asleep (most probably) in her seat or basket, you won't be sure what you should or shouldn't be doing. And why would you – you've never been in this situation before.

I would suggest that rather than reading the paper, posting a status update on the social network of your choosing or firing up the PlayStation and shooting stuff, you should make yourself look busy in some way, as a nod to the fact that you know a storm is approaching. Tidy things up. Make sure everything is where it's supposed to be.

Keep looking at your watch for no apparent reason. And while you do all of that, keep reminding yourself that what unfolds as soon as your baby wakes up won't actually be as tricky to deal with as you are fearing, for the simple reason that, at this age, babies are very simple, uncomplicated souls.

As we'll discuss in greater depth as the book goes on, all newborns need to do for the first few weeks is sleep and feed and poo and cry. Sleep and feed and poo and cry. Sleep and feed and … On a loop, seemingly ad infinitum.

Your job during these first twenty-four hours and then beyond is simply to be there to take care of everything that needs to be done. One midwife put it nicely, telling me and my wife that our new job when our babies arrived home was to 'just keep them alive'. Did I say nicely? I meant terrifyingly. But she was right, that is all you need to do and the job starts here, in these first twenty-four hours.

Treat this time as a chance to simply find your feet, to work out what's what and how it will all work. Soon, in fact as soon as over the page, you'll need to start thinking about establishing an all-important 'pattern' for your baby, a routine for happier living. But that is not for now. These first twenty-four hours are a case of simply surviving. Close the curtains, take the phone off the hook and don't bother answering the door. Take stock and simply concentrate on getting through.

ESTABLISHING 'A PATTERN'

The key to a happy, healthy childhood, or so
they say . . .

Many experts talk of the need to establish 'a pattern' as soon as possible, by which they mean getting your baby into a feeding and sleeping routine that quickly becomes regular and consistent. Everything else fits in around this routine, including nappy changes, baby interaction and every other part of your new life. Establish a workable routine and your baby will very quickly be sleeping through the night, feeding like a dream and growing up to be big and strong and important. Or so the theory goes.

Failure to establish a pattern can have dire consequences – your baby will scream every night and sleep through the day, refuse food and go on to fail all his exams, and this will be entirely your fault. Or so the theory goes.

Now there's more than one way to establish a pattern, but what seems to work well for many is to remember the very basic rule that your newborn baby needs feeding every three to four hours. Some babies need more food than others, but that rule applies to most. And if you stick to that rule, everything else falls into place around it.

For example, instead of seeing the day as twenty-four hours, night and day, you can break it down into a series of feeds – say, 10 a.m., 2 p.m., 6 p.m., 10 p.m., 2 a.m., 6 a.m., and so on around the clock.

If you feed around those times, and factor in a nappy change and full hygiene service after each feed (as that's when babies tend to magically open their bowels), your baby is likely to then go back to sleep again until his next feed. Because as you'll see in the early weeks, babies do little else but sleep, eat and soil their nappies.

And so there, as if by magic, you have established The Pattern, or at least A Pattern. It won't always work like clockwork and there will be times when your baby wants an extra feed, but as a general rule that seems to work for many new parents, this '10-2-6' plan makes a lot of sense.

Your baby will be happy in a routine, and you – the parents – will be able to work around him in the time you have, doing things like tidying up, shopping for nappies and quickly shoving a sandwich down your throat without tasting any part of it. The reassuring thing is that most parents find things get easier after three months. That's something to look forward to . . .

Handy Man

Just a quick word on the vitally important subject of making yourself useful. If you don't already pull your weight around the house, once your baby has arrived and has taken up residence, you will certainly need to. Indeed, even if you are handy and helpful now, when Junior arrives you will need to become truly indispensable.

This means you will need to wash clothes, do the washing up, the shopping, the cooking, hanging out the clothes to dry, putting the dry clothes away, paying the bills, all the general fetching and carrying that needs doing and just keeping the house tidy ahead of a constant stream of guests arriving at your front door.

In truth, you'll need to be doing everything you should have been doing before your baby came along, plus much more. Live by the simple rule that 'There's Always Something Needs Doing', and never go upstairs or downstairs without something in your hand, because once you have a baby, everything is always in the wrong place.

Most crucially of all though, make sure you do what needs doing *without being asked to do it*. It makes all the difference.

BONDING WITH YOUR BABY

How to strike up a strong bond with your newborn baby...

By most, if not all, accounts, the best and easiest way to form an intimate bond with your new baby is by feeding her the milk she needs, because this allows you to establish eye contact and coo at her up close.

Sadly for you, if your partner breastfeeds regularly, your work here will be limited as you don't have the correct 'equipment' for breastfeeding. Watching mother and baby connect so effortlessly can leave you feeling unneeded and unloved, but given the benefits of breast milk, only a fool would complain.

And besides, there are other really good ways that will help you establish the essential daddy–baby bond. I can think of the following six examples:

1. Changing Nappies

An obvious suggestion but this is a key role made for the man who isn't afraid to quite literally get his hands dirty.

2. Winding Your Baby

While your partner is feeding, be on hand to take care of ridding your baby of any windy air pockets as and when required.

3. Rocking Your Baby To Sleep

Post-feed and post-winding, you can play another essential role. The pungent aroma of bosom milk all mums carry about them can stimulate even a just-fed and brim-full baby, making it hard to get her off to sleep. You, however, smell only of man musk so are far better placed to *very gently* rock your baby off to sleep. (*Very gently* because she will be full of milk.)

4. Talking To Your Baby

Either through reading books or just having a (one-way) chat about stuff. Your baby won't understand a word of it until she's around six months old, but talking gently to her will help her recognize your voice. Point out simple things in books or around the room and you're also helping develop her vocabulary.

5. Playing

It could be said that as most men are only overgrown toddlers themselves, playing comes very easily. In years to come, this may involve going in goal or carting them around on your back like a horse, or a wheezing donkey. For now, it will likely mean shaking a rainbow-coloured elephant with unrealistic mirrored ears. This 'light play' is a vital part of your baby's development and a very easy way to bond.

6. Bottle Feeding

There will be times when your baby won't be able to feed on the breast. Sometimes pre-bottled breast milk will be required, or you'll offer them a bottle full of formula. Either way, that is when you can enter the equation and make those big doe eyes, so be patient and bide your time.

THE COST OF RUNNING A BABY

*There's no way of sugar-coating this: raising a
baby doesn't come cheap . . .*

According to a recent report, the cost of bringing up your child until
he reaches the age of twenty-one is £218,024. You probably think
that comma's in the wrong place and that it should read £21,802.40.

But it isn't. And it doesn't. It reads £218,024, a figure so steep it
could turn a dad to drink, if only you could afford it.

And of course, if you have twins or you have another baby
down the line, as many people do, you will obviously be looking at
significantly more, particularly when you factor in inflation and the
fact that in the time it's taken you to get this far, the cost will have
shot up again.

Broken down, you're looking at £10,400 a year for a single child,
or £865 a month, or £28.44 a day, every day, until he turns twenty-
one and gets a job, if there are any jobs left to get. (And if there aren't,

then you're looking at considerably more than £218,024, but we can worry about that later in life.)

Now, even though those figures have been put together by someone working in the Worst Case Scenario Department, someone instructed to 'put absolutely everything on the list and let's just see what it comes to', there's no denying that running a small person will be a costly business, particularly in his first year when you'll need to buy all manner of stuff to set him up for the years ahead.

As you progress through this book you'll see a number of suggestions for the essential kit you'll need – ranging from nappies and bum cream, up to the bigger contraptions such as buggies and beds. They're all entirely optional, because there really is no right or wrong way of doing this, but aim to offer some kind of enlightenment.

What it's probably most important to say is: You don't have to buy everything they pressure you into thinking you need. Selling unnecessary products to panicking parents has become a boom industry, but less is often more in the first year. I'd suggest you only need The Essentials that are dotted throughout the book.

The Kit: Some Stuff You Probably Don't Need

There are a million ways to waste your money where baby products are concerned – type 'potty trainer iPad holder', 'baby poop alert' and 'bacon-flavoured infant formula' into Google and marvel at the nonsense they claim will benefit your baby.

Of course, they are the more extreme options but the baby market is awash with stuff that will supposedly make your baby happier and your life easier, but probably won't.

According to a recent survey by a leading consumer-advice organization, the following ten products are entirely unnecessary and should be struck off every parent's shopping list.

1. **Fabric sling** – to wrap your baby up and hang him from your chest

2. **Nappy stacker** – a system designed to keep nappies in good order

3. **Baby washing** (top and tail) **bowls** – for washing your baby's face and bottom

4. **Nappy disposal bin** – for disposing of nappies

5. **Bumbo seat** – a plasticy-rubbery seat designed to help your baby sit upright

6. **Door baby bouncer** – a contraption for hanging your baby from the door frame and allowing him to bounce up and down for a while

7. **Baby carrier** – a more advanced alternative to the sling

8. **Ride-on toddler board for buggy/pushchair** – for when you have more than one child and walking won't do

9. **Night light** – a light for the night, for babies being trained to fear the dark

10. **Baby reins** – to make your child think he's a dog

Now you may find some of those products actually work for you but the message here is simple: don't be hoodwinked into buying everything out of panic. A newborn baby needs a lot, but far less than you might think.

CLOTHES AND ASSORTED KIT

*When bringing up a baby, some things really
are essential . . .*

The previous chapter outlined some of the things you really don't need to buy as a new parent. This chapter reels off the bare essentials you absolutely will need. So let's start with the clothes on your baby's back.

The Clothes On Your Baby's Back

Now as much as you might want to dress your baby up in a pink tutu with angel wings or tweed three-piece to emphasize their individuality, for the first few weeks all any baby usually wears is a basic wardrobe of just a few fairly plain items. Initially, the emphasis should be on functionality over frills.

As she grows bigger you'll obviously need to expand her wardrobe (see page 37), but from Day One you'll only really need the following:

- **6 Babygros** for both day and night. These are all-in-onesies with strategically placed popper buttons that make it swift and simple to put them on and take them off.

- **6 pairs of socks** to wear in the night if it's cold or to wear when you venture out. Socks get lost very easily, so maybe get more.

- **4–6 vests.** For warmth when it's cold or to be worn on their own when it's warm, and as added protection against leaky nappies. That's the beauty of vests.

- **2 cardigans**, preferably light ones as they allow you to build up layers to get the temperature just right.

- **A blanket** to wrap your baby up and keep her nice and warm … yes, you get the picture.

- **A wool or cotton hat**, some little mittens and a pair of baby bootees for going out if the weather is cold.

- **Several pairs of scratch mittens**, because your baby will end up scratching her face as she thrashes around in her sleep, unless she dons the mitts.

- **A winter coat** or a lighter baby coat if it's supposedly warm but all very changeable.

- **And a sun hat** for going out when or if the sun shows up.

Next-Stage Clothes

After the first few weeks you might want to start moving away from dressing your baby in mainly nightwear and upgrading to proper people clothes, albeit in tiny sizes.

Unless you have no friends on the planet, or no friends who have already had a baby, then much of this next-stage clothing will be handed down to you by parents who have been there and whose babies have almost instantly outgrown their clothes.

It's quite possible that you won't have to buy a single piece of next-stage baby clothing as you will end up being given more than enough to get by. And as your baby gets bigger, the babies ahead of them will keep getting bigger, so the clothes should keep on coming.

Of course, you could be snobby about using cast-offs but your baby will grow so rapidly that buying a Lacoste polo shirt or fur-lined Ugg boots that become too small overnight is, in truth, a waste of money.

Interestingly, and weirdly, it's been said that if your baby kept growing at the rate she does in her first year, by eighteen she would be as tall as Nelson's Column in London – which is fifty-two metres high. Getting clothes to fit her would be impossible and while it's an unverifiable stat, it illustrates the speed your baby will outgrow her wardrobe. I'd suggest the money you spend on expensive baby clothes could be better spent on something worthwhile – a holiday, for example, or a bigger car.

Now, how you choose to dress your baby is entirely down to you and I can't advise you on what to buy, except to say that it's probably better to have just two or three showpiece outfits for your baby to wear when you want to parade her in front of friends, relatives and heads of state.

It's better to buy little but often and keep the tags on each item until you use it and the receipt safe, in case you're better off just taking it back if it doesn't fit.

Also, be guided by the seasons – don't buy an arctic coat for your baby to grow into in six months' time if, in six months' time, it's the middle of summer. Or vice versa.

Moses Basket

Also known as a bassinet, so for clarity: this is a lightweight but durable little bed/cocoon for your newborn baby to sleep in. It's initially better, and smaller, than a cot because you can carry it around the house and it should be good for the first three or four months of your baby's life. It should come with a set of bedding and a foam mattress and more expensive models come with a nice wooden stand on which the basket sits, as if on display. This isn't necessary and your baby won't care if she's placed on a stand or the floor, but do make sure it has two stout handles as they'll allow you to transport your sleeping cherub from A to B and back again, ideally without ever waking her up and making her cry like a baby.

Swaddling Blanket

A way of wrapping your baby up for bed, this clever blanket stretches tightly around her at bedtime, mimicking the feeling of being back inside the womb and giving her – and so you – a better night's sleep. Some require loads of fiddly folding, others have been designed so that even a fat-fingered dad can wrap the baby almost effortlessly. They're entirely optional and only good for the first month of your baby's life, but I certainly would use one.

Cot

When your baby outgrows her Moses basket, you'll need to move her into a cot. However, you need to think several steps ahead when choosing your cot. Look for one with removable side and end panels that extend its life well into your baby's toddling years. A height-adjustable base and drop-down sides for easier access are also well worth considering. A teething rail for when your baby wants to chew something without causing damage to the cot or her gums is also a nice addition, but not essential. And be aware that baby bumpers that are designed to sit in the cot and prevent her from getting her arms caught in the bars have been banned in the US for being a danger to your baby. Just something to bear in mind, that's all.

Travel Cot

An essential piece of kit for when you finally escape the four walls of your house as a family. The name is the giveaway here. It's a cot, but one cleverly crafted using a series of cranks and pulleys that, when activated, see it spring fully formed into a standing baby bed in a matter of seconds. And when you're ready to depart the next day, you simply press the same button and marvel as it collapses in clever, controlled fashion before folding up into a small, easy-to-transport box, just small enough to be shoved into the boot of your car. The reality is that you'll spend far longer than the packaging blurb claims pulling and pushing at the legs until they slide kind of but not quite into place, so it pays to try before you buy.

Baby Monitor

Big Brother for babies: the monitor is a two-piece walkie-talkie – one half sits close to the cot, the other half sits near you, allowing you to listen in to your baby's gurgling from the comfort of a room elsewhere. The moment you hear the first strains of a cry coming down the line, you can hot-foot it upstairs (assuming you have stairs) to offer assistance, unless you're watching TV and it's at a critical point and Junior can wait. Seriously, leaving your baby to cry for 'a bit' doesn't make you a bad dad. By 'a bit' though, we're talking a couple of minutes rather than an hour and a half. Also, some more expensive monitors feature in-built cameras so you can watch your baby rather than the TV if there's nothing on, or if you're just really, really paranoid.

Toys

On those rare occasions when your baby is not sleeping or feeding, she will almost certainly demand some kind of entertainment. Which is where toys come in, and where you discover that it's a very fine line between an overpriced piece of plastic tat and an essential tool for your baby's first learning experience.

Because everything in the outside world is new and exciting to a tiny baby, you'll notice that she quickly becomes obsessed with things she can pull at and push, scrunch and squeeze. It's all about sensory overload in the first year and your baby will be drawn to bright toys that move and things that make a sound, which is why baby mobiles clamped above the cots that pipe out nursery rhymes will never go out of fashion.

In the early weeks, your baby's eyesight is the least developed of her senses and she can only see about ten inches in front of her. She also can't grasp things for herself, so she'll take great pleasure from you holding a bright toy that squeaks or scrunches close to her face. The sounds stimulate her brain while bright, contrasting colours help her pick out the shapes and patterns.

You might also like to introduce a small mirror to the equation – to amuse you and confuse your baby when she spots her reflection for the very first time.

By around three months, when she becomes completely obsessed with grabbing things, tactile toys and fabric books become increasingly important for stimulating her curious mind. Baby gyms, activity centres and padded mats with arches that dangle toys above them to push and prod can occupy your baby for ages, helping develop her grabbing and grasping skills and allowing you to enjoy a brief moment of calm reflection.

Having said all that, where toys are concerned, the truth is that your baby will probably be as happy with a piece of reflective, crinkly kitchen foil or an empty packet of baby wipes as with an expensive toy that's been hand-whittled by an artisan toy maker in a workshop in Wales. Particularly as, from four months on, all babies become obsessed with investigating their hands and their feet.

But, because playing is all part of a baby's mental and physical development, it's probably worth investing in toys designed specifically to stimulate and gently educate, just in case it helps her grow up to be a genius.

Whatever you buy will be dictated by budget, and you obviously won't be stuck for choice. Just make sure it's completely safe, with no sharp edges or small parts that come loose, and no strings that can get caught around your baby's neck or fingers while you're not paying full attention.

TRANSPORTATION

*How to get your baby from A to B safely –
and then back again . . .*

The first few days of your new life as a dad (and mum, and new family) will probably be spent staring at the same four walls of your house, trying to make sense of it all and keep things under control. Soon though you will probably want to venture outdoors as a family, for the sake of your vitamin D levels if nothing else.

You'll probably need to go to the shops to get more nappies or you might just want to venture out into the world to show your baby off to family, friends or random old ladies in the street. (Just as an aside, be warned that if you choose to walk anywhere, accept it will take twice as long to get there than it would if you were without a baby. My wife couldn't get ten paces down our road without pensioners waddling over to ''ave a little look' at two sleeping babies. One memorable old woman peered in, said to my wife, 'Ooooh, poor cow, you've got your hands full!' and then waddled off again. And while that turned out to be true, we didn't need to be told on Day Three.)

However you choose to travel – on foot, in your own car or via public transport – you'll need the most suitable transportation device.

And in an overcrowded market, you'll need to choose wisely and know what's what.

On Foot: A Baby Carrier or Sling

For the parents who walk a lot, both carrier and sling do a similar job. The carrier is effectively a fabric baby bag that fits to your chest, with adjustable straps to keep your baby securely in place. He can face your chest if he's asleep, or away from you when he's awake and wants to see where he's going and all the stuff going on around him. Most are suitable up until about a year old and babies like them because the close contact they get from being tucked up close to your body reminds them of being in the womb. It makes them feel warm and protected and makes you feel like a kangaroo. Which is never a bad way to feel.

Because carriers are hands-free, you can carry your baby yet still move about more freely and get on with doing whatever needs doing – sending a text or shopping in the supermarket. And here's a real bonus: when out and about, the sight of a new dad with his newborn baby clamped to his chest is pretty much guaranteed to draw admiring glances from all the womenfolk you pass. This vision suggests to them that you are a thoroughly modern man, a hunter-gatherer alpha male who remains in tune with his nurturing instincts. You probably aren't either of those things but let them think it anyway as you head for the oxtail soup.

Meanwhile, the sling is a sheet of fabric that essentially wraps your baby into place against your body, once again giving him the sensation of being squashed inside his mum's tummy. However, a spate of deaths in the US of babies carried in slings means I'm certainly not going to suggest you use one here. And on top of all that, slings are better suited to breastfeeding mothers who appreciate the discretion its fabric folds provide than for a dad like you, who will just end up looking like a substandard cowboy.

A Set Of Wheels: Pushchairs

Here you basically have three options: a Buggy, an All-terrain Buggy or a Travel System. Each have their merits, and can be summarized like so:

Buggy

Aka 'strollers' and available in all sorts of shapes and sizes, from the lightest, most basic model to more robust builds that have been pimped with all mod cons. As a result, buggies appeal to most people. Just be aware that some strollers are not suitable for babies under six months old as the backrest doesn't recline far enough and there's not enough of the padding your baby needs. Ask the nice salesman before purchasing, and keep the receipt.

All-terrain buggy

Like a regular buggy, but designed for active parents who like to take their baby up and down hills and on beaches and who aren't perturbed by the odd adverse camber. The trade-off is that because of all that clever cushioning and the fatter wheels, they are often more expensive and larger than a standard buggy, making them harder to drive round shops or on public transport, pack into the boot of your car, or store under the stairs when not using. But hey, life is a compromise.

Travel system

The most convenient option, but often more expensive as a result. For 'travel system', read 'Transformer', for this is a clever contraption that cleverly morphs from a child car seat into a buggy-type stroller at the flick of a few switches. The real beauty, as you'll soon recognize, is that you can transport a sleeping baby all over the place on various modes of transport without bothering him (i.e. waking him up). Also, when not in use, the wheel section can be folded down, making it easier to store in a boot or cupboard. The only downside is that this may encourage you to leave your baby in his car seat for longer stretches, which is not good for his physical development.

Three Key Questions

When buying wheels, consider the following before handing over your debit card . . .

1. The cost

Only you can define what is good value and what represents an extortionate rip-off, so there is no right and wrong on cost. There are well-regarded buggies available for £150 (and less if second-hand), and there are models right up to £1,000 that are also considered, by some, to be money very well spent. Only you can decide. All I'll say is that, as with fine wines and quality footwear, you do tend to get what you pay for, particularly if you'll be using it a lot.

2. What's included

When buying a pushchair, be sure to check what's included in the price, so that you have the full picture. For example, check whether you will have to pay more for extras such as raincovers, footmuffs, accessories bags, bumper bars and go-faster chevrons down the side. And be aware that what the smiling salesman has failed to mention is that with travel systems, the price rarely includes the child car seat.

3. Storage

If your house is a squash and a squeeze, considering storage is crucial when buying a new set of wheels. Will it fold down small enough to store out of sight? If not, this is not the buggy you're looking for. Measure up before you go shopping, and insist on a full demonstration of any model you might be thinking of buying.

Three Key Considerations

Because we don't all need the same thing . . .

1. If you mostly walk

You should look for a pushchair that's easy to push on a variety of surfaces and can negotiate kerbs and stairs with ease. Good suspension and large wheels will result in a smoother ride, but if you'll be walking on rougher ground, an all-terrain pushchair is a better bet. Protection from wind, rain and sun is also important and if you or your baby's mum frequently have to negotiate stairs with the pushchair, you should choose a lightweight one or risk wheezing like a donkey every time you go out. (However, depending on the distances you cover, you might decide you want a baby carrier rather than a set of wheels – see page 43.)

2. If you mostly take public transport

You should look for a pushchair that's lightweight and folds as small as possible at the flick of a switch, because buses in particular are full of miseries who tut under their breath. (The folding mechanism is key with much of this equipment – you'll need something that will fold with as little effort as possible, preferably with one hand or the controlled knock of a knee.)

3. If you mostly drive

Then it sounds pretty obvious you'd be best off with the full travel system. That said, make sure whatever you opt for will fit in your boot before you buy, rather than learn the hard way, which will most likely be when it's lashing down and your patience is in very short supply.

Car Seats: Rules And Regulations

If you only read one entry in this whole book, make sure it's this one, because choosing the right car seat is a matter of life and death. If you're travelling in a car with your baby, by law they have to be strapped into a car seat. It is illegal to carry them in your arms, even if it's a really short journey and the car's being driven really, really slowly.

When buying a new seat, look for the United Nations ECE Regulation number R44.03 or R44.04, which are apparently the gradings that guarantee safety and peace of mind. In the coming years, both grades will be replaced by a more fashionable sounding i-Size grading, but that remains in the pipeline at this stage. To be sure you have the right type of seat, always ask the most sensible-looking salesperson in the shop or research fully online. Car seats are not an area where you can afford to take any short cuts.

As a basic guide on the sizing front, be aware that car seats can be labelled either as Group 0, Group 0+ and 1, or as Stage One and Stage Two. The grouping label is more common but you'd be better off and safer if you choose the right seat based on your baby's weight. Here's a guide:

Weight range	Approximate Age Range	Group	Stage
Birth to 10kg (22lb)	Newborn to 9 months	0	1
Birth to 13kg (29lb)	Newborn–18 months	0+	1
9kg to 18kg (20lb to 40lb)	9 months to 4 years	1	2

Depending on how fast your baby grows, his first car seat can last up to two years before it needs to be upgraded to a more advanced seat designed for older babies and toddlers, though it's safest to be guided by weight more than age.

One very easy rule to remember though is that you'll need to upgrade the minute you notice your baby's head poke above the top of his current car seat – or when it looks like that moment won't be far away. Also, make a mental note to check for signs of wear and tear in the seat as time goes on and replace when necessary. As a general, if vague rule: remember that they don't make them like they used to. Though actually, where baby seats are concerned, that's no bad thing.

In terms of the style of seat, recent advice to parents that I'm now going to parrot states that children should travel in rear-facing car seats until they are four. Stringent tests have shown that rear-facing seats offer greater protection to tiny infants in the event of a crash and also provide the vital support your baby's head and neck need in his early months. A rear-facing car seat, for the uninitiated and the easily confused, is one which sees your baby facing the rear of the car, rather than facing front as you will be.

The important, no exceptions rules

■ Ideally, your car seat should be new, not second-hand. If it is second-hand, you'll need to be absolutely certain that it's never been involved in a crash before, as that would compromise its ability to protect your baby.

■ It needs to fit securely into your car and sit sturdily without wobbling as you drive – another reason to try before you buy. It should come with a 'head hugger' (a little built-in pillow) as standard (as your baby has no neck control until he's three months old).

WARNING!

Ready And Able

If you leave the hospital by car, you will need to show the hospital staff that your car seat is in full working order and that you can put your baby in it safely. This should be all very simple but familiarize yourself with the parts and process so that you don't end up fiddling around in front of the nice nurse. Also, make sure you understand fully how the car seat fits into the car because it will probably be raining when you leave the hospital and after giving birth, your partner will not want to sit around for an hour while you get confused by the instructions.

The important (but not absolutely vital) rules

- Look for a model that detaches from its base, allowing you the option of transporting Junior on foot or transforming into a travel system when you want or need to leave the car. Given that most of the time your baby will be fast asleep in the seat, not waking him up is a key consideration.

- Look for a model with sturdy yet somehow comfortable handles, otherwise your hands will end up bruised and your arms will feel like they've been yanked clean from their sockets. Even a small baby plus seat can weigh very heavily.

- Look for a seat that's designed to rock gently when you take your baby out of the car, allowing you to rock a crying infant back to sleep, or keep a sleeping one snoring for hours on end. (Given how much time he will spend asleep, the rocking option is a nice addition, but remember that infant seats can leave your baby squashed and place a strain on his developing spine if he spends too much time in it. Unless you want him to grow up looking all bent out of shape, limit the amount of time he sleeps in it.)

DADVICE Every Cliché Is True

Those first few days were tough for a number of reasons. There was always the ever nagging question 'Is that normal?' Should he sleep like that, should he sleep this little, should he cry this much? In time it makes sense but during those early days you just don't know what's right and what's wrong. The crying was always my biggest concern before he was born – the not knowing what to do to make him stop. It feels at the time like it will never end and it brought me to tears a few times, but like everything, it gets better. The best advice I can give is that every cliché fits. It's a phase, they are all different, they change your life, you will look back and laugh. It's all true. Equally, everyone has their story of having a child. Your stories are the memories you will keep for the rest of your life.

PAUL H, LUCAS'S DAD

PART TWO

A MASTERCLASS IN THE
DILIGENT DAD'S DAILY DUTIES

SLEEP

There ~~may~~ will be trouble ahead . . .

As even the most ill-prepared of new dads will have heard, your newborn baby will be getting loads of sleep in the opening weeks of her life, and you will be getting next to nothing. But this is hardly news.

The whole lack-of-sleep-you'll-feel-like-hell thing is a cliché because it's true, but it doesn't matter. Yes, you'll feel more jiggered than at any other point in your entire life, and at times you'll want to curl into the foetal position and sleep for a month, but your paternal instincts will kick in and remind you that you are now doing the most important job in the world. And besides, sleep is overrated. Four hours is all you need, provided you crank yourself up on fierce coffee and don't operate heavy machinery for a living.

As hard as it might seem, and as clichéd as this will sound, the sleep deprivation bit really is just a phase. You simply have to keep reminding yourself that this is about as hard as it gets and it never gets this hard again. And it does have an end. Two months, maybe three, and then it gets slightly easier. But let's not get too far ahead of ourselves here. Let's go back to the start and consider some numbers.

Newborn babies sleep for as many as eighteen hours every day, which means they're only awake for six, which all sounds pretty manageable. The only problem is that they never sleep those eighteen hours through in one go because their sleep at that age is broken into smaller chunks of 'REM' sleep (so called because it occurs at intervals during the night and is characterized by rapid eye movement and bodily movement). So, as a general rule, you can expect your baby to get two hours here, three hours there, possibly four if you've truly been blessed.

WARNING!

Frayed Tempers

Be forewarned that the lack of sleep and high levels of stress can cause parents to bicker and snap at each other. Even if you had the most loving, rock-solid relationship imaginable before Junior arrived, you may soon end up arguing over trivial nonsense. Tolerance levels will be at an all-time low and words may be said that sound blunt, possibly even brutal. If she calls you a very rude word in the middle of the supermarket because you left the shopping list at home, she's just very tired and probably still in a lot of pain. She probably doesn't mean it. It's just the stress of the situation coming out, and if you're being honest, you know she's right. Don't take it personally. You will get back on track as things calm down and you'll eventually look back and laugh at this tricky spell, providing you don't say anything you can't later apologise for. Like everything, it's just a phase.

Working round this pattern through the day is no real problem, because parents are generally awake during daylight hours and a baby who's awake is more entertaining than a baby who's still asleep.

But it's during the dark hours that it becomes more of a problem because as the man of the house, and a man who will probably go back to work after two weeks, I'd suggest that your job is to be on call for your baby. And that means round the clock, all day and every day, including weekends and bank holidays.

Which means you too will be surviving on smaller chunks of 'REM' sleep, dozing very lightly and with one eye open. Initially, at the slightest sound, you will spring like a ninja from your bed, ready to take care of whatever emergency has arisen. After a few nights, your spring will have been replaced by the leaden-footed trudge of a man getting by on three twelve-minute chunks of sleep a night.

But every day after three months, every night should get slightly easier. From six to eight weeks on, most babies start to sleep for longer during the night and move from shallow, REM, liable-to-wake-in-a-funk-any-moment kind of sleep, to a deeper, more satisfying slumber. This means your baby will be awake for longer during the day and demanding more of your time, which is an excellent trade-off.

Hold on to the thought that from as early as four months in, your baby could start sleeping twelve hours at a time through the night, if you're really very lucky. However, you'll need to accept that this could take nearer five or six months and it won't happen every night. And because your body has been reprogrammed to serve and protect and jump out of bed at any slight noise, you'll find yourself jumping out of bed multiple times every night at the lightest cough or gurgle. But slowly your baby is progressing towards sleeping like a fully functioning human being should.

I won't mention that I'm still woken in the night to attend to vitally important tasks such as locating small fluffy teddies they're lying on and moving the pillow slightly to the left or to the right, or that my boys are now five, because at this stage, that won't be very helpful. Think only positive thoughts and say this repeatedly: After three months, it does get easier.

18°C

The supposed safe temperature for a baby's room is anywhere between 16°C and 20°C. You can establish the temperature by investing in a room thermometer, but be warned that if the temperature drops below or rises above either extreme, a buzzer will go off in the local police station and a van will be sent to cart you off to jail.

In reality, as long as your baby doesn't look or feel too hot or too cold, and as long as you employ some rudimentary common sense, such as adding clothes in the cold and removing them in the heat, you should be just fine. A St John Ambulance man once told us that 'babies should always feel a little bit cold around the edges', so if their chest is warm and their hands a little cool, that's OK.

Six Helpful Sleep-Related Questions And Answers

1. Where should my baby sleep at night?

In your bedroom, either in a Moses basket or a cot. Never in your bed, with you, as you could very easily squash her. And never near a radiator or heater, as this could raise her temperature and cause the uncommon but still highly disturbing Sudden Infant Death Syndrome, aka SIDS, aka cot death.

Some parents will keep their baby in the same room for the first full year and more, others will move them into their own room after as little as the first few days. Whatever feels right for you is the correct answer here, because there are pros and cons to both options.

Having your baby in the same room can put your mind at ease that she's safe during the night, and not being kidnapped by a fox or choking to death on your parental paranoia. But having your baby in the same room can flick your mind onto high alert, and every little cough or splutter can have you hurtling out of bed to check everything's all right. Your baby being in the room next door won't guarantee a peaceful night's sleep as a result, particularly if you have a baby monitor, but the distance can be helpful and it will feel like you're making progress.

2. What should my baby sleep in?

Most likely a sweet little all-in-one Babygro, with or without a vest underneath, depending on the season and the weather at the time. Common sense is the key here, but one rule of thumb a lot of parents (OK, a lot of mums) hold true is to dress your baby in clothes you'd be warm enough to sleep in, then add one extra layer. That, they say, would be about right. You might also want to swaddle your baby – but that's covered on page 38.

3. What should my baby sleep under?

Most likely under a combination of cotton sheets and cotton cellular blankets, at least for the first few weeks. Using these light, individual blankets makes it easy to regulate the temperature, which is absolutely completely crucial during the dangerous first year because of the threat of cot death. For that reason, duvets and pillows should not be used at any point in the first year as they pose a significant threat of suffocation.

To avoid your baby overheating, check the temperature by all means but never at the expense of using common sense and parental intuition. If your baby feels too warm she will attempt to push her covers off and may even assume the sunbathing position – arms and legs flung out to the side. Depending on how well tucked in she is, this may not be possible for her to do, so an easier check is to touch her head or tummy to feel if it's hot or sweaty. If it is, remove clothing or layers until she feels more comfortable. And if she feels cold, add layers and so on. But never use her hands or feet as a gauge as they can often feel a little cooler by default.

After a few weeks, you might want to put your baby to bed in a sleeping bag – a baby-size sleeping bag that fits neatly over the shoulders and removes the problem of her throwing off the blanket in the night and starting to cry as a result. More importantly, as long as you have the correct-size bag for your baby and it fits as it should, it also removes the danger of her wriggling down under the covers and overheating. Some bags are designed for winter and feature a higher 'tog' rating, others are designed for summer with a low tog. Here's a handy guide:

Room temp	Bedding	Sleeping bag
24°C or more	Sheet only	0.5 tog
21°C	Sheet + 1 blanket, or 1 tog sleeping bag	1 tog
18°C	Sheet + 2 blanket layers, or 2.5 tog sleeping bag	2.5 tog
16°C	Sheet + 3 blanket layers, or 2.5 tog sleeping bag + 1 blanket	2.5 tog

Note: Be aware that a single blanket folded over equals two layers. Oh, and if like me you were wondering, the 'sheet' is the thing that covers the mattress, the 'blanket' covers the person sleeping in the bed. Important to clear that up.

4. How should my baby sleep?

Like the proverbial baby, you'd hope. In terms of how she should literally sleep, the safest position for your baby in the first year is to always sleep on her back. She should be positioned so that her feet are at the bottom of the basket or cot, with the bedding placed securely and no higher than her shoulders to keep her in place for the night. This way, she is less likely to wriggle under the covers and get into difficulties.

5. How much sleep should my baby be having at night?

As much as she needs is the only answer, but the following is a rough guide:

0–3 months: Eight to eighteen hours, but spread throughout day and night. She will wake (you) up when she's hungry, or feeling hot or cold.

3–6 months: Eight hours or more at night. At some point here she'll be spending more time awake during the day.

6–12 months: Twelve hours at night, as much as fifteen over a full twenty-four hours. The night feeds will have been phased out, but teething and the associated issues can kick in here.

6. People talk about establishing a bedtime routine. What might that involve?

From around three months, you can introduce a bedtime routine that should help your baby understand the difference between night and day and establish a very solid sleeping pattern. This should help her sleep longer through the night, which will help you sleep longer through the night, which constitutes a win–win for everybody. The routine should start when she gets sleepy at around 7 p.m. and include the following, in order:

1. A bath

2. Change into bed clothes

3. Drink milk

4. Brush teeth, if there are any teeth to brush

5. Into bed with the lights on low

6. A bedtime book (something gentle, nothing dramatic)

7. A kiss goodnight, a few words to say it's time for sleep, and you exiting while she's still awake. This final step will probably result in tears the first time (see Controlled Crying, page 64), but in time it will become easier. It's important your baby learns to fall asleep in her cot by herself, rather than in your arms while you strangle a lullaby and whittle a rod for your own back.

The idea here is to establish a simple pattern your baby associates with bed, so when she gets in the bath she begins to automatically wind down for the night. Now is not the time for Fun Time Daddy – now is the time to be a cool, calm and composed cat.

Eight Signs Your Baby's Tired

You – not your baby – should control when she goes down for a sleep, but recognizing the signs that she's feeling tired is a good Jedi skill to master. Look for these signs:

1. She yawns and stretches a lot

2. She repeatedly rubs her eyes

3. She flicks her ear with her hand

4. She stares blankly into space

5. She yawns again, this time more dramatically

6. She goes very quiet and still

7. She becomes noticeably grumpier – whining at the slightest thing

8. She's already fast asleep

Note: Also check the time in case she's already falling into a sleep pattern.

Controlled Crying

This comes in from six months as a way of teaching your baby to understand that it is time for bed and that she needs to go to sleep because you have to put the house back together. It will probably break your heart a little bit but pays off in the long term.

The idea here is to establish a routine and set some parameters, with the ultimate aim of teaching your baby to sleep more routinely through at night.

Basically, you put your baby to bed awake, then leave the room. This will almost certainly trigger tears, which you pretend you can't hear as you stand outside the door feeling very guilty. You return after a few minutes to check she's OK, remind her in a stern, schoolmasterly voice that it's time to go to sleep, then leave the room again.

This process continues, with the time spent out of the room increasing incrementally. It may take five minutes or it may take several hours, but eventually your baby will fall asleep.

The following night, you repeat the process until by the end of the week (with any luck), your baby is able to settle herself. Each subsequent night should get slightly easier, though it may get worse before it finally gets better and your neighbours may end up calling the police.

Note: Only attempt this if you can dedicate a full week to it – there's no point having two nights on, one night off as it sends mixed messages. Also, don't attempt this if your baby is ill – otherwise her cries could be more serious and this becomes a dereliction of parental duties.

HOLDING AND CARRYING A BABY

Get it right and it's a breeze.
Get it wrong however . . .

Just as there's more than one way to skin a cat (thirty-four, apparently), there's also more than one way to safely hold your newborn baby. Four obvious ways, I would suggest, and they all have one absolutely crucial thing in common: each makes sure your baby's head and neck are fully supported. Until your baby reaches around four months, he won't have the strength to do this for himself so you <u>HAVE TO</u> do it for him, without fail.

In time and with practice, you'll work out which works best for your baby – he will usually let you know by looking happy or by going to sleep instead of crying at you. So, in no particular order:

The Cradle

The classic, textbook hold. It involves placing your baby's head in the crook of your preferred arm, with the other arm wrapped securely and comfortingly over his body. With your baby lying down, put one hand under his neck first, then pick up round the back of the legs and move into place. Many babies would happily sleep for hours in this position, but after ninety minutes you'll have lost all feeling in your holding arm so you should think about putting him in his cot soon after he's fallen asleep.

The Upright

This is much the same as the technique for burping/winding your baby (see page 122). Pick and lift as with The Cradle, but then place your baby facing you against your chest, to whichever side of your neck you prefer. His little head should just be poking over your shoulder. Support the

neck with the high hand and carry the weight under his bottom with the lower. You're right: this is almost insultingly easy. Just wait for the next one.

The Lap

For when you don't need to be standing up or moving around, you simply sit in a comfortable chair with your knees propped up slightly. Lay your baby face up along your legs, with the back of his head resting against your knees and his feet on your toned stomach/ sprawling gut. This is best for when your baby is awake and you want to interact by putting your face close to his and making a series of wibble noises.

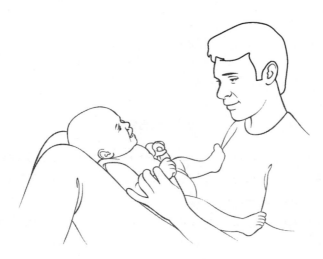

The Belly

You bend your stronger arm to ninety degrees and then lay your baby's chest down along the underside of your forearm. His head should be resting to one side in your hand. Bring the arm in to your body, use your free arm to secure him in place, then gently massage your baby's back. This is slightly more advanced than the previous holds and comes with the added risk of dropping him onto the floor, so attempt with caution.

WARNING!

Not that you would, but **never ever shake your baby**. Newborns and young babies have no control of their head and neck so even the slightest shake can cause significant damage – in severe cases leading to brain injuries and death. Proceed at all times with extreme caution.

DADVICE · Make It Up As You Go Along

Once your baby's home, the best advice is to ignore all the advice you've been given. We humans are pre-programmed to deal with every situation and you will work it all out.

Also, it's a cliché, but just enjoy it. Visit zoos, jump in ball pits, watch kids' TV, eat pizza, play with toys, read silly books . . . Sleepless nights, baby sick and tantrums are not the things you will remember – your mind will be rewarded with lovely super-8 film montages with glorious soundtracks that cleverly edit out all the bad bits.

Before I had kids, I never understood why grandparents always looked so happy around their grandchildren. I now know why . . . they've been given the chance to do it all again.

RICHARD B, LAUREN AND OLIVER'S DAD

CRYING

Why won't it stop? Why is it so loud? And is it OK for you to cry too?

It's an unfortunate design flaw that babies have no magical mute button or batteries to take out. If your baby is crying – and a lot of the time she will be – then something is not quite right.

Your job is to play Poirot and find out what sort of not-quite-right it happens to be – and then work out what to do about it.

In time and with experience, identifying the problem will become a breeze. In the first few days, though, you probably won't have a clue.

So with that in mind, here are twelve likely causes, plus some possible remedies:

Has She Filled Her Nappy?

In extreme cases it will be apparent to everybody within a fifty-foot radius if this is the case. If there's no obvious stench, you'll need to pick her up and take a good, deep sniff of her bottom. You might feel a little uncertain about doing this at first, but soon it will become second nature and you'll be sniffing her backside just because you can and that's what dads do. Change the nappy, if required, and the crying may stop.

Is She Hungry?

Even if your baby is in a nice, well-established feeding pattern, where you think you know when she'll want milk, she can still sometimes get hungry early. Think of it like this: just because you know you'll be having your dinner at 6 p.m., it doesn't mean you don't fancy a biscuit at 4.15 p.m. Luckily, a hungry baby will give off signals to show she wants milk, which those in the business call 'rooting'. To avoid a rooting baby reaching the crying stage and becoming far less reasonable, you'll need to recognize the signs early. If she's breastfeeding, call her mum. If she's not, ready a bottle.

Is She Too Hot Or Too Cold?

If your baby has a temperature of 38°C or more when aged three months or less, or 39°C aged between three and six months, she has a fever. If she is just a little bit hot or cold, add or remove a layer of her clothes, turn the heating up or down, open or close a window, use the brain in your head. If she looks and feels sweaty, there's a good chance she's a bit too hot. If she's too cold, the icicles on her nose should give it away and you'll need to add layers.

Is She Just A Bit Bored?

Possibly. And really, can you blame her, being cooped up in these four walls for twenty-three hours a day, listening to grown-ups wibble and coo and the sound of that *Breaking Bad* box set? If you suspect it's boredom causing the tears, she may just need some entertainment. And you are the cabaret. It's time to send in the clowns! Actually, cancel the clowns – they'll give her nightmares for life. Instead, go through the following options:

The cuddly toy

Introduce for a little light mirth, shaking it gently and close enough to her face that she can see what it is, but not so close it scares the life out of her. Never whip her into an excitable frenzy or she may get hysterical and be sick.

Take a walk

If lighter stimulation is required, simply walk around your house (or wherever you are) and explain to your baby what you're doing and what you can see, providing you can't see anything obscene, like the man across the road getting out of his shower or a tramp being sick in a bin. A change of scenery is often all it takes. Your baby can't talk back but if she falls silent and seems to be in awe, it's doing the trick.

Sing a song

Find a tune your baby likes – 'The Grand Old Duke Of York', 'Old King Cole', 'Hickory Dickory Dock', 'Who Let The Dogs Out?' The only real rule: croon gently – any rambunctious noise will likely alarm her and cause more tears.

The pick up

Your baby may just be craving some close contact. After nine months inside, squashed up against her mother's innards, she's become used to feeling snug. You could swaddle her (see page 38), but that's better deployed for when sleeping. So your best bet is to just give her a cuddle and whisper sweet gobbledygook into her ear. If this doesn't work, it might help to pass her to someone else. Sometimes she just doesn't want you, she wants her mother. Deal with it. Hand her over and go and make her mum a cup of tea.

Rub her tummy

Sometimes the canine in your baby will make her want a gentle tummy rub. Nothing complicated, just a gentle rub to soothe her back to happiness. For some reason, this very simple technique often works best in the night.

Has She Become 'Overstimulated'?

Sometimes, there's just too much going on in this new and exciting world around her, so your baby can quickly get confused or feel overloaded by the sights and sounds and just start blubbing uncontrollably. You may also feel this way during the first few days and weeks, but while you need to pull yourself together, your baby will need to be soothed. Relocate to more sedate surroundings and read to her in low, soothing tones until she stops crying and probably falls fast asleep.

Does She Need Burping/Winding?

If during feeding your baby swallowed down a load of air, possibly because you didn't feed her in an upright position, then that air will be rattling around her innards, trying to find a way out. It may exit through the back door but it's more likely you'll need to burp (or wind) her to set free all that air in a series of amusing baby belches. (See page 122 for a full outline.)

Is She Simply Feeling Tired?

Despite having slept almost solidly for the past twelve days, she could well be crying because she's a bit tired. If none of the above possibilities seem to apply, or if you know from your baby's sleeping pattern that at this stage she probably shouldn't be awake, you'll need to gently rock her back off to sleep. And here's a curious thing: you apparently rock side to side to soothe a sleepy baby, and back and forth to amuse and stimulate. Hey, I don't make the rules.

Is She Teething?

They say this doesn't usually happen until around seven months or so, but sometimes even 'They' can get it wrong. Even if there's no sign of a little toothy peg poking through, the teething process may have begun. The symptoms – drooling, gnawing their hands or toys, a fever, a face or chin rash, diarrhoea and many more – can kick off from as early as three months, so even if there's no sign of any pearlies as yet, there may well be signs. The bottom front teeth usually come first, and the gum will start to look an angrier shade of red. Teething rings, teething gel, cool drinks and the ubiquitous infant suspension mixture can all offer quick relief.

Does She Want Her Dummy?

Often the simplest and most obvious solution. If you've chosen to pacify your baby with a rubbery dummy, apply it now and enjoy the sound of instant silence. If you already did apply the dummy but it's no longer there, find where it fell, give it a clean and reinsert it, or replace it with a new one and carry on doing what you were doing before the crying began.

Does She Have Colic?

Ah yes, that severe, often fluctuating pain in your baby's abdomen caused by intestinal gas or an obstruction in the intestines. It affects one in five babies, and if your baby is the chosen one then you are, in a sense, a bit jiggered because she'll cry uncontrollably, even if she's otherwise completely healthy. No matter what you try, it won't make the crying stop.

Colic usually kicks in at around three weeks and crying in colicky babies typically begins in the late afternoon/early evening, when they start to get a bit tired and ever so irritable, as we all do.

Look for the telltale signs: a colicky baby will have a red face and flushed cheeks, she'll draw up her legs, possibly arch her back, squeeze her fists into tight, angry little balls of fury and ignore your futile attempts to reason with her by waving that furry little toy in front of her face.

The precise cause of colic is unknown, and there is no guaranteed cure, though swaddling, offering a dummy, gently swinging your baby in your arms (side to side), and a delicate tummy massage are all said to help, but consult your doctor first and so on and so forth.

Like all things though, colic should just naturally pass, usually around the four-month mark, six months tops. Can you survive on no sleep for three to six months? Sure. Just start drinking quadruple espressos.

Rapid Response

Leave your newborn baby crying for any length of time and she will feel ignored, which will make her cry louder, which will make her confused and possibly angry, which will cause her to cry louder, and the pain caused by her crying louder will probably cause her to become apoplectic with confused anger that will make her quite possibly explode.

Your baby's crying is her only form of communication. As a child she will talk, as a teenager she'll grunt, but at this stage she has no option but to open her lungs and strip the paint off the walls.

Answer her promptly (a few minutes is OK) and she'll apparently grow into a happier toddler than a baby left to cry and cry and cry and cry.

Note: *Having said all of the above, it's still fine to try Controlled Crying (covered on page 64) when your baby is six months or older.*

Is She Ill?

If you suspect your baby could have an illness, despite you having no formal qualification as a GP, you'll need to act fast. Generally, expect a weak, nasally cry, one that in its own way is telling you she just doesn't have the energy to muster anything louder. Diagnosing an ill baby is a subject important enough to warrant its own entry on pages 85–93.

Does She Have Some Other Complaint Not Covered Here?

She very easily could have. Or he, if he's a boy, as many baby boys end up crying because they somehow get a human head hair wrapped around their winky, so it could be that. It could also be a hair wrapped around a finger, scratchy clothing tags rubbing them up the wrong way, just being a bit uncomfortable or even not liking the music you've put on, or the programme on TV, or the strength of the light, or any number of other diva issues that will make you feel like JLo's dad must have felt when she was growing up. Pity poor Mr Lo.

Important note: Studies have found that babies usually cry more in the evening than during the day, largely because, like you, they get tired as the day wears on, but unlike you they can't prop themselves up with caffeine. Be aware that some perfectly happy babies cry themselves to sleep. If they do this regularly and your doctor has checked that there is no other factor involved, you have nothing to worry about. Most importantly of all, they say most baby crying tends to slow down around the three-month stage, so ring that as a red letter day on the calendar.

White Noise

Oddly, many babies calm down and stop crying when they hear the sound of the vacuum cleaner or washing machine. Some people who have tried everything else also recommend typing 'white noise' into YouTube and hitting play. It often works.

The Crying Code

Not all cries are the same and it's often possible to identify the problem from the sound and style of your baby's shriek . . .

Hunger Short, high-pitched, slightly desperate cries that rise and fall, as if your baby is pleading for food.

Pain Sudden, louder and longer-lasting, followed by silence as she fills her lungs and prepares to cry again. She'll likely thrash around while doing this.

Overtired A breathy, slightly nasal cry that can be intermittent but builds steadily until she has had enough and really opens her lungs.

Sick Often very nasal and weak, a sign that she can barely muster the energy to cry properly.

Boredom Starts with short bursts of noise, including laughter, as she tries to instigate a 'conversation'. Expect full crying if you fail to react.

DILEMMA

THE DUMMY

To Plug Or Not To Plug, that is the question – and one of the greatest dilemmas facing confused parents in the first few days. To bring in the dummy and feel like you might have failed in some way? Or to struggle on heroically without one as your baby cries you to the edge of insanity?

Only you can decide which way to go and nothing I write here should sway you, but I'll say that dummies are magnificent if you're looking for a quick and easy way of calming your baby. They bring instant relief for both the parent(s), the baby and, in extreme cases, the next-door neighbours. So how can that be wrong?

The big problem with dummies is that relief is only ever temporary and as soon as the dummy is spat out, falls out or is removed, the noise is likely to start up again, particularly if your baby has grown accustomed to sucking on it.

So the dummy can become a lazy habit and it can soon become much easier to lazily shove the plug back in than find out what's causing the crying in the first place. Also, babies who suck dummies all the time grow up to have buck teeth and get laughed at in the playground, although there's no real evidence to back that claim up.

What has been proven though is that breastfeeding babies shouldn't use a dummy, and particularly not in the first month when you're looking for them to gain weight, as excessive sucking can confuse them. It's also been proven that your baby won't learn to fall asleep for herself if she relies too heavily on the artificial stimulant of a dummy. And if she does get to sleep but wakes in the night to find it's fallen out, you can expect to be woken from your light slumber by her piercing screams. And as you fumble around to find it in the dark, and then finally shove it back in, you'll know that you'll be going through the same charade again a few times more before this night is over.

In its defence, alongside the fact it offers a quick fix, you can argue that sucking a dummy is preferable to your baby sucking her thumb, because you can't take a thumb away in the same way you can remove a dummy. Less in its defence is the fact that some doctors claim that prolonged dummy use can apparently cause ear infections, for reasons I wouldn't even pretend to bluff my way through here. So there are pros and there are cons. But like everything in life, moderation is the key. If used sparingly, in short bursts when you have no other choice, the dummy can be your new best friend. Using it won't turn your baby into a serial killer in later life and it doesn't make you a bad dad for applying it, as long as you're not just taking the easy option so that you can read the newspaper in peace. As long as you wean your baby off it by three to six months, a year at the very most, then all should be fine.

Cranial Osteopathy

A peculiar one, this. Cranial osteopathy is either the miracle cure for a baby's dreaded colic, which if eradicated can lead to less crying and a better night's sleep for your baby and you, or it's the type of new-fangled healing hands nonsense they never had back in the old days when parents just grinned and got on with it. Which one it is really does depend on who you talk to.

Either way, the theory goes that your baby's delicate body can be pushed, pulled and twisted all out of shape during childbirth, leaving kinks and tension that causes them understandable discomfort. In fairness, you too would be irate if you'd just been pulled head first out of a tight passage and might well complain.

Your baby can't complain and so takes the only option open to her: she cries, long and hard until you take some sort of positive action. If you're so inclined, you may employ the services of a fully qualified osteopath, whose highly trained hands will be put to work eradicating the kinks causing the discomfort. To do this, he or she applies very light but very controlled pressure to your baby's body to feel for these strains that are causing the pain, and then gently works them free using techniques I don't even pretend to understand.

All I do know is that many babies have been shown to sleep far better after treatment, which in turn helps their parents sleep better as a result, which suggests it's money very well spent. But, well, many babies haven't been shown to sleep any better after being gently pulled this way and that, so consider the jury still out on this one.

DADVICE Follow Your Instincts

I was in shock after we had our first baby. I knew something absolutely amazing had happened but I was genuinely in a daze. The hardest things for me were the sleepless nights, trying to juggle work and not having a clue what you are meant to do with a newborn baby. I mean, what is 'normal' behaviour for a newborn? I – and we – really had no idea. Luckily, you learn very fast to go with your instincts. I also wasn't prepared for how vulnerable they are and how reliant on you they will be, but you learn quickly that they are surprisingly resilient. The best advice I can give is to make sure you remember to enjoy them as they are absolutely amazing and they grow up all too fast.

MARTIN T, EMILY, BERTIE AND RUPERT'S DAD

ILLNESSES AND AILMENTS

*The common and classic illnesses and
ailments likely to bother your baby in the
first year . . .*

Your baby will get ill. As inevitably as death, taxes and imminent rain, there is very little you can do to stop this happening. And the reason is simple. When your baby is born, he's protected by a special immunity that acts as a kind of superhero force field, protecting against bacteria and viruses.

He's given this gift during the last few months of being in the womb and it's added to when he drinks breast milk – nature's ingenious way of protecting him against the filthy outside world with all its sickness and woe until his immune system cranks into gear.

Sadly, after a few months this magical cloak of invincibility loses its power and leaves him open to a wide range of ailments and illnesses. Some will be nothing to worry about, others will need a trip to the doctor or hospital. The tricky job is to work out which reaction is required.

What became clear early on in our circle of new parents was that the mum and dad often take very different positions where illness is concerned. While new mums fret constantly that every little splutter or red patch is the first sign of a life-threatening illness that needs urgent medical attention, many dads will often shrug and suggest we just 'keep an eye on it'.

The two approaches dovetail quite nicely. The mum is on a permanent state of high alert and first-name terms with the emergency services switchboard operator, the dad offers a more balanced, optimistic assessment, even though he has absolutely no medical training whatsoever. As a result, you're likely to meet in the middle and be about right.

That said, a little insight into the most common illnesses and ailments you'll almost certainly encounter in the first year cannot hurt, so here it is, starting with a fact and a warning:

36.9°C

This is the normal temperature of a healthy baby. But because the figure will vary slightly depending on who you ask, take your baby's temperature when he is happy and seemingly well so that you have a reference.

WARNING!
Know Your Limitations

It almost goes without saying that if you're in any doubt about an illness, ailment (or indeed injury), call the doctor or emergency helpline at the earliest opportunity and ask questions later. Reassuringly, during the first few days and weeks, and then at regular intervals thereafter, your baby will be in 'The System' and will be inspected by all manner of doctors, nurses and assorted health visitors. Anything untoward should be picked up fairly quickly, but vigilance is a parental prerequisite.

Colds

Symptoms The common cold, for which there is no cure, is so common that you'll quickly get used to the sight of thick mucus streaming from your baby's nose.

Cause It's usually just a mild viral infection causing the membranes of the nose and respiratory passages to swell and deposit snot.

Treatment Steam can help loosen the congestion and let him breathe easily again. One method is to turn the shower on to really hot, let the room fill with steam and sit with your baby in the bathroom (NOT in the shower) for a few minutes. A few menthol or eucalyptus drops on his bedding will also help. If this fails and he's under three months old, call the doctor. If this fails but he's over three months, give it a week to pass – unless the mucus becomes thicker and more yellow, or breathing becomes a problem, or the cold becomes a fever, or his lips or nails turn any shade of blue.

Conjunctivitis

Symptoms The whites of your baby's eyes will look red and inflamed. It will start in one eye but soon spread to the other. His eye(s) will be more watery than usual, may become puffy or swollen and a substance best likened to thick mucus may loiter in the corners of the eye(s) when he wakes up after a sleep.

Cause Inflammation of the conjunctiva of the eye – the conjunctiva being the thin skin that covers the whites of the eye. There are several reasons for conjunctivitis striking but the most likely is due to bacteria or a virus.

Treatment Many people leave it alone and hope it goes away, and often it does as your baby's tears contain clever chemicals that wage war on the infection, but it may take a couple of weeks. Bathing the eyes with cool, clean water helps. As with all things medical, it's best to check with your doctor first to make sure it's nothing more serious and so he or she can prescribe the right drops. And be aware that it's highly contagious, so wash your hands regularly unless you fancy a dose yourself.

Better Safe Than Sorry

Never give your baby any medication you are unsure about or which hasn't been checked by the doctor first. Aspirin, for example, should never be given to a baby as it can cause life-threatening Reye's syndrome. Always double check anything before giving it to your baby and always stick strictly to the dosage suggested on the packaging.

Constipation

Symptoms Your baby unexpectedly stops going as regularly as you've grown accustomed to – fewer than three brown deposits a week is cause for concern. This can be combined with a loss of appetite and a hard, tight stomach.

Cause There's likely a blockage caused by a bulky stool that will not shift. This is more common in formula-fed babies and can often be caused by feeding the wrong dose of formula or by changing brands.

Treatment Only you can decide if the level of discomfort needs an immediate call to the doctor. If your baby is formula-fed and you suspect it's just a light blockage with no underlying issues, give him plain (boiled, cooled) water in between feeds. Make sure your formula measurements are as they should be. And employ a favourite trick to loosen stools of gently pedalling his legs forwards or backwards – the movement can often dislodge the blockage.

Note: If you spot blood in his nappy or suspect it's severe constipation that is causing significant pain, call the doctor.

Diarrhoea

Symptoms It's officially diarrhoea and not just common poo if it arrives more frequently and in a more liquid form. It can also be accompanied by vomiting and a fever. The colour and smell will be noticeably different (see page 142 for details).

Cause It's usually a virus but can also be caused by milk intolerance or a resistance to antibiotics.

Treatment In simple cases it should firm up within forty-eight hours – if it doesn't, or if your baby shows any sign of becoming dehydrated as a result, call the doctor. (Symptoms of dehydration include no wet nappies, lethargy, dry eyes, a dry mouth and a sunken fontanelle; cooled, boiled water between half-milk, half-water feeds helps avoid dehydration.) Also see the doctor if you spot blood in the nappies, your baby also has a high fever or he seems in any pain.

The Fontanelles

What sounds like a close-harmony band from the 1950s is in fact two soft spots on a newborn baby's head. The bones of your baby's skull have not yet fused together so there are two soft spots, one on the front of the head and one towards the back – the fontanelles. They close naturally after six weeks and eighteen months respectively and are usually nothing to worry about.

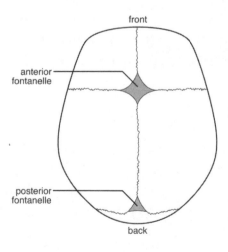

Fever

Symptoms Your baby will feel so hot you could make toast within five inches of his face. Babies often get hot but a fever takes hot to disconcerting extremes – any temperature over 37.5°C is considered a fever.

Cause It could be dehydration, it could be overdressing your baby in a warm environment, or it could be there's a virus brewing and your baby's immune system has turned up the heat to fight it off.

Treatment If the temperature is borderline, remove items of his clothing, cool the room down by opening a door or window, and keep him hydrated. A dose of paracetamol for babies three months and over will also help. Give it time and it will often just pass. But seek medical help if your baby is:

(a)   Younger than three months old and has a temperature of 38°C or more.

(b)   Aged three to six months and hits 39°C or above.

(c)   Over six months old, has a fever and shows other signs such as being drowsy or floppy.

Ear infection

Symptoms This will likely start with a cough or a runny nose and build to a fever three to five days later – a classic ear infection pattern. But there are others too: your baby waking up in the night but not wanting a feed, pulling away from his milk, seemingly being in pain, cantankerous, refusing to lie flat and just generally being out of sorts – they can all be signs, but there are so many it becomes tricky to spot. Ear infections are very common in babies, particularly in the winter months.

Cause Most likely a cold, which results in your baby's middle ear becoming swollen and causing significant discomfort due to trapped fluid in which bacteria and viruses can do their dirty work. Other causes can include bad feeding technique, dust flying round the room and smoke from the cigarettes of irresponsible adults.

Treatment Luckily, many ear infections sort themselves out within three or four days. However, if you're concerned, ask your doctor nicely and he or she may well prescribe some fast-action antibiotics.

Gastroesophageal reflux

Symptoms Numerous, including frequently bringing up food (often within a couple of hours of being fed), frequent crying, poor sleeping, being irritable and refusing to feed. Telltale signs include your baby pushing his legs up and arching his back during or after a feed.

Cause The acid in your baby's stomach regurgitates back into the oesophagus and causes all sorts of discomfort. It's common up until around seven months, but is often passed off as colic (see page 75), which it isn't.

Treatment Feed less but more often and with your baby in a more upright position, as this reduces reflux and increases the production of saliva, which neutralizes stomach acid and lubricates the oesophageal lining. Call the doctor if this doesn't do the trick or if your baby appears to be in too much discomfort. And hang in there: the condition should improve as your baby moves to solid food.

Vomiting

Symptoms The contents of your baby's stomach suddenly appear without warning and it's more than just a posset (see page 123).

Cause If it happens straight after a feed, you may have simply overfed him, or you have fed him and then bounced him around on your knee too much. If it's not that, it could be the result of a cold, a reaction to a certain food or a bug or infection, particularly if he's been hanging around with other babies.

Treatment The odd quick vomit is nothing to worry about if your baby seems otherwise healthy and feeding as usual. It should pass within twenty-four hours and if it does, Code Red can be downgraded to an Amber. It should be more of a concern if it doesn't pass with twenty-four hours, or if it's accompanied by any of the following symptoms:

■ Your baby is vomiting with great force

■ The sickness is accompanied by a fever – with floppiness, sleepiness, irritability and a loss of appetite

■ Your baby is showing signs of being dehydrated – a dry mouth, noticeably fewer wet nappies than usual. Keep him hydrated as much as you can because what comes out will have to be replaced

■ His breathing has become more difficult

■ His vomit contains streaks of red or green – caused by him coughing up blood or bile

■ He has a bulging fontanelle (see page 88)

If these symptoms don't pass within twenty-four hours, or if you just want the reassurance that it's nothing to worry about, call your doctor as soon as possible.

Meningitis and septicaemia

Symptoms Feared by all parents, and understandably so as both can be life threatening if not picked up early. The symptoms can be similar – pale, blotchy skin, blue lips, cold hands and feet despite a raging temperature (39°C and over that won't shift), and your baby's cry being strangely high pitched. With septicaemia, a red or purple rash may also develop, with small spots at first, spreading and becoming blotchy and looking like bruises.

Cause Usually a bacterial or viral infection for meningitis, and a blood infection with septicaemia.

Treatment See the doctor as soon as humanly possible.

For anything else

The following symptoms are widely regarded as being serious enough to suggest you seek urgent medical attention:

1.   A noticeably different cry – be it high-pitched, weak or one that won't stop.

2.   A noticeable lethargy, drowsiness or reduction in energy, particularly if your baby is unresponsive, seems floppy or struggles to stay awake when he ordinarily would be.

3.   A bulging fontanelle, front or back (see page 88).

4.   Not taking on fluids for more than eight hours. This is more of a concern than not eating.

5.   Repeated vomiting, or vomiting that appears bile-green.

6.   A temperature of more than 38°C if your baby is under three months old, over 39°C if three to six months, and above 40°C if older than six months.

7.   A high temperature combined with cold feet and hands.

8.   Turning noticeably pale, or blue or particularly spotty. A spotty, purple-red rash anywhere on the body could be a sign of meningitis.

9.   Irregular breathing, be it fast or struggling for air. Check for your baby sucking his stomach in

Who To Call

For mild concern: Call your doctor. If it's out of hours, they should have a number for emergencies.

For rising concern: As above, but your nearest hospital's accident and emergency ward should be an option for things like raging fevers, lethargy despite taking medication, breathing difficulties, severe abdominal pain, or proper emergency issues like dangerous cuts or broken body parts.

For significant concern: Call an ambulance if your baby is struggling for breath, has stopped breathing, won't wake up or is unconscious or unaware of anything that's going on, or if he has a fit, even if he then seems to recover. All of these predicaments should be considered an absolute emergency.

Immunization

At various stages of your baby's first year, the doctor will jab him with a sharp needle and fill him full of terrible diseases, including such classics as diphtheria, tetanus, whooping cough, polio and meningitis. This is not as bad as it sounds – these jabs put a small dose of the disease in so that your baby's immune system starts to produce antibodies to fight it off. It will make your baby cry, which might make you cry, but the dose will protect him if or when he's exposed to that disease in the future, so it has to be done. The jabs come early – usually from a couple of months on, and your doctor should be in touch to arrange an appointment. Any further questions, ask your health visitor or phone your doctor direct and play dumb.

Note: *Your baby might well develop a light fever after these jabs. This is perfectly normal and known as post-immunization fever. It can be treated with a drop of paracetamol-based infant suspension.*

At Death's Door

In an act of great solidarity with your baby, every time he picks up any kind of illness in the early months, you will often end up getting a hefty dose of it yourself. At least that's how it was for me and every other dad I know – we all became more ill than ever before when our babies arrived, particularly when they went to nursery and started hanging around with other bite-sized bug-spreaders. The mums rarely caught a single thing, oddly, but the men dropped like flies. It was like a heavy man flu you just couldn't shift, and it's lucky none of us brave dads died.

It's odd because unlike your baby's immune system, your own should be up and running properly by now so it should be able to fight off any illnesses that take a fancy to you. I'm guessing the high stress levels and sleep deprivation leave us wide open to it, but I'm not medically trained and I can't explain why the mums seem more immune to it. All I can do is offer a solution: to avoid catching anything from your baby, simply move out for the first two years of his life and only communicate via letter. Too extreme? Then just avoid kissing, cuddling and any other close contact with him between the ages of five months and two years. No? Then all you can do is accept that you will get ill. Suck it up, stop complaining and hope that your boss is also a dad – a great advantage when you're constantly phoning in sick.

DADVICE Embrace The Chaos

The biggest surprise of parenthood to me was the almost total loss of any leisure time, or time for yourself. And I don't mean struggling to squeeze in a four-hour round of golf, I mean drinking a cup of coffee while it's still hot, and the basics you take for granted. Everything else in your life comes second to your baby and you have to adapt.

I'd also say just getting out of the house was hard, in terms of the planning required before even getting into the car or being ready to walk down the road. Getting the timing right is key – has the baby been fed, is he good to go, ready for a nap? Have you got everything you need? Milk? Snacks? Water? Nappies? Wipes? Spare clothes for him? Spare clothes for you? Dummy? Back-up dummy? It's exhausting.

Don't stress too much if things don't run like clockwork in the first six weeks. It will be chaos and there's no way of avoiding that. Just embrace it and let life turn upside down for a while. It's a completely new phase and won't last for ever. The structure will kick in after a couple of months and by a year, it will all have become much easier.

KEVIN H, JOSEPH AND ESME'S DAD

COMMON AILMENTS

Now these are not serious enough to be classed as 'sick', but there are still several ailments that can be a cause for concern.

Jaundice

If your baby's skin looks a little yellow in the first few days, it's most likely jaundice. This is caused by the build-up of bilirubin in the blood, bilirubin being a yellow substance produced when red blood cells are broken down. Jaundice is common in newborn babies because they have a high level of red blood cells and these are broken down and replaced frequently. The liver in newborn babies is also not fully developed, so it's less effective at removing the bilirubin. The good news is that it can and usually does just pass on its own within a few days, although it can get slightly worse before it gets any better. The baby's drinking of milk (breast or formula) will help flush out the bilirubin. Ask your midwife or doctor if you are at all concerned.

Baby acne

Your baby may get an attack of face pimples during the fourth or fifth week. This is nothing to worry about and is caused, probably, by overactive oil glands in the skin. It will pass a damn sight quicker than the zits he'll get as a teenager, but you can speed up the process by washing your baby's face with a very mild soap every day.

Nappy rash

A common complaint in the first twelve months, and understandably so. If you were to sit around in a pair of big sealed pants containing poo and piddle, your delicate skin would also start to look angrily chafed as well. However, your baby's skin can also look red and sore if it's simply overly sensitive or allergic to a certain type of soap or cleaning product. Best practice here is to change his nappy frequently, so he's not left sitting in waste for any length of time. It has been said that a newborn urinates every twenty minutes, then once an hour by the age of six months. Luckily, modern nappies are designed to lock a baby's waste water away, but as a rough guide, aim for around twelve nappy changes a day in the first few months. Clean the affected area with plain water and leave the nappy off whenever possible so the air can get to your baby's bits and work its magic. Finally, to speed up the process, apply a nappy-rash cream to the sore bits. If it still doesn't clear up after all that, or it gets a brighter, angrier shade of red with pimply bits, and it spreads into the folds of your baby's skin, it could be a more serious fungal infection. See the doctor for a jar of his special anti-fungal cream.

Cradle cap

You'll probably know this as seborrhoeic dermatitis, which means your baby's head is red and flaking, as if he has a heavy dose of dandruff. Unless it turns particularly severe it's nothing to worry about. Most cases pass naturally after the first year, but heavier doses can stick around stubbornly. There are a number of anti-seborrhoeic shampoos available, but I speak from experience when I say none of them worked. My son's head developed a terrible crust, but none of the shampoos we tried made any difference. Then a really good doctor suggested smearing a drop of olive oil on his scalp before a bath, washing his hair as normal and then gently combing the loosened skin out with a fine-toothed comb afterwards. That worked a treat and he now has a mane so glossy it might one day win an award.

Teething

As early as three months in (but at any point in the first year), your baby's first teeth will start to push through his gums. As you can imagine, this will cause pain and result in an irate baby until all twenty teeth have finally broken through, which can take up to two agonizing years. The signs are usually pretty clear: red, irritated gums, flushed cheeks, excessive dribbling, biting down on anything he can get his teeth on, wetter poos, and a possible rise in temperature.

Teething gets a very bad press, in that babies are often very irate during this time, but it's sometimes less the teething and more the fact your baby will be around the six-month-old mark, which is when the special magical illness immunity he had from birth begins to run out and he starts picking up every illness known to mankind. You'd be irate too if you were feeling ill and your gums were exploding.

But relief is at hand in various forms. A water-filled teething ring is the simplest trick – it's designed to be chilled in the fridge and then have the life chewed out of it. Cold water also helps, and helps rehydrate your baby if he's been dribbling excessively, as many do when they're teething. Dipping your finger in cool water and massaging his gum also helps, and may make you feel a bit like Tony Montana in *Scarface*. There are also various homeopathic teething granules available, if you're alternatively inclined.

ESSENTIAL KIT
INFANT SUSPENSION

This is a paracetamol-based, fruit-flavoured painkiller that you might want to call upon when your baby is unwell or uncomfortable but not enough to bother the doctor. Commonly administered for headaches, toothache or teething, sore throats, cold, flu, fevers and following jabs when your baby will be feeling peaky, it is quite possibly the best thing you can buy in a bottle – even better than any kind of alcohol. Shake well, use sparingly, always read the label and so on and so forth.

HYGIENE
(HOW TO KEEP A BABY CLEAN)

How soon is too soon to bathe a baby?
Sooner than you'd think . . .

Your newborn baby can have a bath from as soon as her umbilical stump has healed (see page 106) – and as soon as you feel brave enough to introduce her to water. The sooner she experiences the bath, the sooner she'll grow to feel comfortable in the water and stop screaming every time you get her wet.

The good news is you don't need to bathe her every single day, unless you somehow have the time or your baby really does work up a whiff come early evening. Bathing every other day or even a couple of times a week is fine until your baby starts crawling – when she reaches that milestone she's likely to get more grubby and need bathing most nights.

Clever parents like you will use a bath to their advantage, introducing it as part of a bedtime ritual. A nice bath can help relax

WARNING!

Now Wash Your Hands

Before we discuss the cleaning of your baby, we need to have a quick word about your own levels of hygiene. Specifically, the fact that when you 'do toilet' you don't always wash your hands afterwards. You were busy and let's be honest, a few germs won't kill you. But, as a new dad, that now has to change. Your baby's immune system is weak and any germs on your hands can easily end up making her sick. So, as quickly as possible, get in the habit of washing your hands thoroughly after every toilet visit. Wash them, apply a moisturizer to prevent them from cracking and bleeding due to all the over-washing you'll now be doing, dry them and maybe even squirt on a hand sanitizer. Two minutes later, wash them again and repeat the whole process. Because you can never be too sure, or too paranoid.

your baby before bed, helping her wind down and making it easier to get her to sleep. So a bath is a good thing. But there are rules.

It should never be rushed. You should never bathe your baby straight after a feed, because fishing baby sick out of the water is never easy, and your baby needs to be awake and in a happy mood, or at least not in a grump or crying. If she's in a grump, being rubbed up the wrong way with a loofah won't lighten her mood much.

The room in which you bathe your baby should be warm, because you don't want her to be shivering, and the atmosphere should be relaxed, comfortable, welcoming and any other hard to define adjectives you can think of. As with everything, preparation is the key and if you have all the bits and pieces you'll need placed around you, you're less likely to be fumbling around when the cleaning begins. I'd suggest the key items are:

ESSENTIAL KIT

A baby bath (or large bowl) filled with warm water. Aim for around 10 cm deep at 36°C, but you can take precise too far. Use your judgement but check the temperature with your elbow.

Baby soap and, if you're using it, shampoo. Be aware that even gentle baby soaps can dry out a newborn baby's skin, so use sparingly.

A sponge or flannel or maybe even one of each.

Two warm, soft towels, preferably one of them with a built-in hood.

Any creams and ointments, should nappy rash arise.

A clean nappy and appropriate change of clothes.

And once these are all in place, close to hand . . .

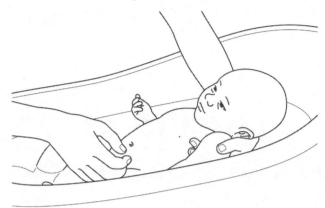

1. Remove your baby's clothes but keep the nappy on. It's easiest to wash the hair first, before she even gets into the bath, so wrap her in a towel, with extra towel 'slack' towards the back so you can dry her hair afterwards.

2. Tuck your baby under your arm, with her face looking upwards and her whole body tipped slightly down so that water doesn't run into her eyes. With your free hand, pour some water over her head, then gently wash before drying with the towel.

3. Remove the towel, remove the nappy, wiping away any lurking muck if required, then place one arm under your baby's back, so her head and back face upwards and rest against your arm between your elbow and wrist. Your hand should have a firm grip on your baby's arm that is furthest from you. With your free hand, support her bottom and legs and gently manoeuvre her into the water.

4. Keep supporting your baby's weight in all the right places (the neck and head, mainly), and support her with kind words and encouragement, particularly if this is her first bath. By now she will probably be bawling angrily and finding the whole process very confusing.

WARNING!

The First Rule Of Bathing Club is also the most important rule: <u>YOU DON'T EVER LEAVE YOUR BABY IN THE WATER UNASSISTED</u>. Never, or Ever. If you need telling why that rule is important, you might not be entirely cut out for parenting. Don't learn this one the hard way. The second rule is that when bathing a boy, never attempt to clean under his foreskin – the skin won't separate from his winkie for several months and your pulling will cause great pain. The third rule is that with a baby girl, avoid spreading any bacteria by always wiping and cleaning from front to back, never ever back to front. The fourth and final rule of Bathing Club is obviously 'No Bombing'.

ESSENTIAL KIT
A BABY'S BATH

You could buy the latest ergonomically designed baby bather in a shade scientifically proven to have a calming effect on a newborn baby's yin and yang and which comes packaged with a thermometer, an additional washing bowl, a complimentary rubber duck *and* a dashing little monogrammed baby robe with hood. Or you could just buy a plastic bowl for £1 or bathe her in the sink. As long as the 'bath' holds water and is clean and comfortable for your baby, you're doing the right thing.

5.   With your free hand, wash your baby gently, working from the cleanest areas into the grimier parts, to prevent spreading it around. Avoid getting the umbilical area wet.

6.   When your baby is all clean, expertly lift her out of the water, then place her onto one of the towels you've put right next to the bath. Make sure she lies down on a stable surface and never try to hold and dry a wet baby off the floor; they can be as slippery as a greased fish and the potential for dropping them is high.

7.   Wrap your baby up warm and pat her dry. Put her clothes on and nod in a very self-satisfied manner that your baby now smells better than she did five minutes ago. Very well done.

The Umbilical Stump

The cord that tied your baby to her mum inside her uterus will have been cut in hospital, leaving just a small stump hanging from the belly button. That's the umbilical stump. It looks a bit like dried meat and probably wouldn't taste dissimilar. Don't be alarmed when the stump turns black, a few days after it was cut, or when it falls off completely – which will be anywhere between a week to a month later. Turning black is normal. You can (and should) speed up the healing process and prevent infection by keeping the area dry and well ventilated. Allow air to get in by folding your baby's nappy down and her vest up, and avoid getting the area wet while bathing. And if the area becomes red, bleeds or emits a worrying stench, cover it up and call the doctor.

ESSENTIAL KIT
BABY WIPES

There are all sorts of products available for cleaning and mopping up after your baby, ranging from cotton-wool balls and tissues for delicate bodily cleaning, right up to muslin cloths for wiping up the more heavy duty vomit, dribble, food, drink and snot. All are highly recommended and very much essential for these early months.

However, the very best product you will buy in the Hygiene aisle will be baby wipes. They are, without question, the greatest product ever created because they will clean anything and everything. Not just babies and their bottoms but also windowsills, toilet seats, the dust now gathering on your PlayStation, the sick on your shirt, wine stains, those grey trainers that once were white and a million other things.

To begin with you'll buy baby wipes out of necessity. But long after your babies' bottoms need wiping and long after they've grown up and moved out, you'll still be bulk-buying these moist little miracles.

Top And Tail

When a full bath is not required, a top and tail allows you to simply wash the bits that need washing. Specifically, your baby's face and neck, bottom and delicates. Clean these using cotton-wool balls dunked in warm water – damp, never dripping; warm, never hot. When cleaning the eyes, use one ball and go from the corner of the eye outwards in one clean wipe, then discard the ball, using a fresh one for the other eye – this is to avoid spreading any infections that may be lurking. Clean the ears in a similar fashion, then clean in any creases of baby pudge around the neck where sweat can collect. Put her clothes back on and move onto the bottom half, cleaning the bottom and the private bits before changing her nappy and applying any cream if any cream is required. That's literally the top and bottom of it.

ESSENTIAL KIT
SCISSORS

Baby scissors are good because they're designed to be almost completely blunt yet still capable of trimming a baby's nails. In truth, baby nails are so soft you could trim them with a butter knife but it's worth investing in a pair of baby's own scissors because if her nails grow too long, she will accidentally slash her own face when your back is turned. And because she doesn't know any better and can't trim her own nails, this will be all your fault.

DADVICE   Ride the Roller Coaster

The first four weeks in particular are a roller coaster of emotions. Initially it's awe – the amazing feeling of just having brought your baby safely home and staring at her, wrapped up snug, still in the car seat, on the lounge carpet. Then shock creeps in. The feeling of suddenly being trapped – especially for the first few weeks, and the inability to just go off and do something at the drop of a hat. Plus there's anxiety. That first time mummy goes to the supermarket, leaving you with a baby. 'Errr, don't be too long, make sure your phone isn't on silent.' And you become quite defensive. Not too many visitors at once – stagger the queues and let the dust settle a little. In time, when you get more confident, it becomes less of an issue, but initially you have to be very protective. My main piece of advice would be just to enjoy every moment because before you know it you'll have a sixteen-month-old and be wondering where the time has gone.

STEVE P, SOPHIE'S DAD

BOTTLE FEEDING

*One little bottle, a billion very
important rules . . .*

First, an apology. The section you're about to read details about as much as you will ever want or need to know about feeding a newborn baby – plus plenty you possibly don't. But given that when your newborn baby isn't sleeping he'll mainly be feeding, this is kind of a big deal. So there's a lot to get through . . .

Unless you possess incredible lactating man breasts, you are likely to be playing a bit-part role in feeding your baby during the early weeks. How much hands-on feeding you will actually get to do depends on how much proper breastfeeding your baby's mum is able or willing to do. If she's churning it out like a dairy farm, you may not get much of a look in and be left feeling unloved out on the periphery while mother and baby make doe-like eyes at each other. This can be hard to take until you read about the importance of breast milk on page 125 and the alternative ways to form a bond on page 30.

But if your baby's mum cannot breastfeed or simply chooses not to, or if your baby doesn't agree that breast is best and refuses to latch on, or if his mum makes up several bottles of breast milk for you to feed to your baby while she is asleep or out and about, or if her supply of mother's milk just runs out, then you at long last will finally get to have a go at feeding your baby.

This is great, because you'll finally feel like you're doing something more useful than just making tea, tidying up and asking if everything's all right. But more importantly, you'll feel like you're forming some kind of close bond with your baby, which you are. But not so fast, because while bottle feeding a baby is not that complicated, there are a number of strict rules and regulations we must cover before you can claim to be qualified. Let's address this in some kind of vaguely chronological order:

When Should I Feed My Baby?

Whenever he shows signs of wanting to be fed is the short answer to this, but it's not always that easy. Generally speaking, small babies need feeding little but often, like a tiny sparrow.

In the first few days, expect him to need milk every two to three hours, then every three to four hours as he gets a bit bigger. During the first week, your baby will need approximately 60–70 ml at each feed; between two weeks to two months, 75–105 ml per feed; and between two to six months, 105–210 ml per feed. By six months it will be 210–240 ml per feed and the total intake could be about 900 ml a day. You'll be able to tell he's getting enough milk by the fact he's getting bigger and wetting his nappies regularly. Remember that these amounts are only a guide. Just as your appetite changes, your baby isn't going to take exactly the same amount each feed so don't force him to finish the bottle. Once you start giving solid food, the intake of milk will reduce gradually.

As mentioned previously, if a baby's not sleeping then he'll probably be feeding – and vice versa – and this is worth repeating because the two things seem to fit in around each other in The Pattern you must now live by.

Of the two parts, establishing a solid sleeping pattern and sticking to it is more important than establishing a cast-iron feeding plan, which means you can and will freestyle on the feeds from time to time. If you're running late for any reason, or if your baby starts to show the classic signs of being hungry, you'll need to react accordingly, not adhere strictly to a set timetable. Remember, it's not about you and all about your baby.

Recognizing the signs of a hungry baby is easy enough, when you know what to look for. When awake, your baby will start moving his head and mouth, looking for something to suck.

An easy and slightly unfair test is to touch his cheek with your finger – if he turns and attempts to suck the life out of it, he's feeling a bit peckish and will need a feed. This is known as the 'rooting reflex'.

So spotting the signs is easy, but spotting them quickly and in time is where it gets trickier. You can't wait for your baby to cry before realizing he wants some food – or at least you can but you shouldn't – because by then it's too late. Crying can often be an advanced stage of hunger, a siren, an irate reminder that you've forgotten to do your job properly.

To stay ahead of the game, make a note of your baby's feeding pattern and always be alert to the signs of hunger. Initially, it might all seem confusing, but after a few days it will be as natural to you as waking up.

Baby Food: What and When

0 to 4 months: milk, be it breast or formula.

4 to 6 months: solids come in, usually fruit and veg mushed into a purée.

6 to 8 months onwards: proper solid solids, such as carrot sticks and toast (depending on how many teeth he has).

What Should I Feed My Baby?

As the box above illustrates, for the first four months or so you'll be feeding your baby breast or formula milk. Formula milk is not the same as cow's milk, otherwise it wouldn't be called formula milk. It's a more complicated powdery formula they sell in cartons and cans down that aisle of the supermarket you'd never been down before you had a baby.

Most babies are happy guzzling first-stage, cow's-milk-based formula, designed to be easy to digest and suitable from birth to around a year.

After a year, second-stage formula comes in and supposedly takes longer to digest. You can switch to second-stage formula after as little as four weeks if your baby is ready, but many babies get saddled with constipation if you switch too soon, and that makes them cry.

You can also feed your baby fresh cow's milk after a year, but don't cut corners and try this any earlier than a year as fresh teat-squeezed cow's milk doesn't contain the balance of nutrients that your baby needs.

How To Feed Your Baby (Part I: Preparation)

As you'll note from the sub-heading, you can't just rush in waving a bottle of milk. Preparation is very much the key where bottle feeding is concerned. The problem with little babies is that they don't yet have a full-strength immune system like you and me. We can eat food straight off the floor and feel no adverse affects, providing it adheres to the strict Five Second Rule.

Babies can't do this because their immune system is still developing, so they can't fight off all the dastardly bacteria that seem to be floating around. Powdered formula, for example, can often contain these little B-bombs that can lead to illness and infection.

So how you prepare your baby's bottle is the key and you'll need to adhere to a very stringent, almost anal policy of sterilizing every single part of every single bottle you use to feed your baby.

Where it says 'sterilizing', it just means 'cleaning every bottle and all its fiddly parts in a solution or a steam-cleaning mechanism until every last bacterium has been eradicated'. It's not complicated, just boring because it becomes so repetitive. But if a job's worth doing and all that, and clearly this is a job worth doing.

How To Sterilize Baby Bottles

Experts say you'll need to be sterilizing your baby's bottles and feeding equipment for the whole of the first year, to reduce the risk of germs developing that could make your baby sick – most likely causing vomit and diarrhoea.

The process begins as soon as you bring in a new bottle – it needs to be sterilized before you use it for feeding, then cleaned and sterilized after every feed and before being used again. Always make sure your hands are clean when handling your baby's bottle or you will defeat the purpose of sterilizing.

Now, your natural reaction after each feed might be to sit around feeling pleased with yourself that you've fed well and without your baby spewing it all back up on you – a combination of pride and relief. Take a moment to congratulate yourself on that by all means, but don't dwell for long because germs multiply at a rampant rate and the longer you leave an empty or half-empty baby's bottle on the side while you sit around, the greater the chances of the germs getting in.

Wash the bottle and begin the sterilizing process as soon as you can. Clean the bottle and teat in hot, soapy water, using a clean bottle brush, then rinse all your equipment in clean, cold running water before sterilizing, which can be done one of three exciting ways:

1. The easy option: cold water sterilizing solution

Put simply, this is a container which you fill with cold tap water and add either a liquid or a tablet of sterilizing solution, which will fizz up and purify the water. Both the water and the tablet need to be changed every twenty-four hours. Once you've thoroughly cleaned each bottle, teat and unscrewable part in hot, soapy water, using a brush to get into all the corners, you'll need to rinse them all clean in cold running water before submerging them in this solution, making sure all the air pockets float out. A floating cover then sits on top of the water to keep the bottles submerged. When the bottles and parts have been submerged for thirty minutes at least, they are safe to use again. Even so, leave them there until you need them.

2. The cheapest option: sterilizing by boiling

As the name suggests, this way involves boiling the bottle and bits in a big pan of water, in the process killing off any lurking germs before they can make themselves at home. Boil for about ten minutes, then carefully remove from the water and piece the bottles back together on a clean surface. Even if you don't plan to use the bottles straight away, piece them back together to stop the inside of the bottle being contaminated. One word of warning though: while this option is the easiest and cheapest, repeated boiling of parts can cause them to crack, so you might need to replace them, making it something of a false economy.

3. The more costly and complicated option: steam sterilizing

The most modern method, which means it's more expensive than the other options, but much easier too. A steam sterilizer is a cylindrical machine that works like a car wash for baby bottles. Generally speaking*, you'll shove some water and several bottles into the machine, plus all the smaller parts, then close the lid and 'cook' the whole thing in the microwave (though there are electric options too) for as long as the instructions instruct you to. Inside, the heat and the water steam the bottles so clean your baby could and will eat his dinner out of them. These bottles remain inside until needed and should stay sterilized for twenty-four hours.

*I say 'generally speaking' because sterilizers vary so much that no single piece of advice will fit all scenarios. Always consult the manufacturer's instructions before you begin, and do read all the small print.

Preparing the bottle

Once your bottle of choice has been safely sterilized for the recommended time, you're finally ready to begin the feeding process.

If the bottle contains pure breast milk, you can progress straight to the 'How To Feed Your Baby (Part II)' section on page 119, because you're good to go. If the bottle needs to be filled with formula milk, you'll need to read this next bit.

Basically speaking, you now need to add water with the powdered formula, cooking up a nutritious milky drink with almost scientific precision.

Carefully follow the quantity guidelines on the packaging – never attempt to freestyle with formula because if you get the mix wrong your baby could end up constipated and dehydrated.

Once you've established the quantity of formula and volume of water required, the process is very simple:

Step 1. Wash your hands thoroughly. Then wash them again to remove any lingering dirt and doubt.

Step 2. Fill the kettle with fresh water and boil it while you ready your bits, so to speak. (Never use bottled water unless you absolutely have no other choice – it contains too much sodium which will cause terrible discomfort.) Shake off excess water from the bottle and teat, which by now you should have taken from the sterilizer. Remove the teat and place on the upturned lid of the sterilizer – do not put it down on any other surfaces – germs lurk everywhere.

Step 3. When boiled, pour the correct amount of water (check the manufacturer's instructions) into the bottle, check the level is right and then add the formula. Dip the dry scoop into the tin, level it off (sometimes formula containers have a convenient 'shelf' inside for this purpose), and carefully tip it into the water.

Step 4. Holding the bottom edge of the teat, which won't come into contact with your baby's mouth or the milk, carefully fix it into position through the retaining ring, then screw the ring onto the bottle. Stick the cover/cap over the teat and shake it like a cocktail until the powder is absolutely dissolved. A handy hint: if the bottle comes with a flat lid, use this (having sterilized it) to shake the mixture and avoid milk blocking the teat. Then remove it and fix the teat on.

Step 5. Because you clearly can't give your baby boiling milk, cool the contents by holding the bottom half of the bottle under cold running water, keeping the cover on to make sure the probably contaminated running water doesn't touch the pure and holy teat. Some clever baby bottles have built-in thermometers to simplify this step, but most don't.

Step 6. Test the temperature of water by shaking a drop onto your inner wrist. It should be warm but not hot. This is why you should never heat the milk in a microwave – the milk may not heat evenly and even if the bottle appears cool, its contents could still be molten.

Step 7. Finally, when the milk is at the desired temperature for your baby, serve immediately, before any bacteria multiply and ruin all your careful preparation.

Note: It's possible and indeed acceptable to make up several bottles in one go and refrigerate what you need for later – just be aware you'll need to use them within twenty-four hours. (As an aside, if storing at room temperature, use within two hours, if stored in a cool bag, use within four.) However, also be aware that the longer you leave a bottle out of its sterilized surroundings, the greater the risk of bacteria building. So it's always best to keep things as fresh as possible by taking it one bottle at a time.

Another note: To avoid having to boil water and wait for it to cool down, particularly when feeding in the dark, cold hours of the night, have boiled water ready prepared and cooled to room temperature or stored in the fridge.

How To Feed Your Baby (Part II: Technique)

And finally we're at the actual feeding stage. This is the section you were expecting several pages ago. Sorry to have kept you, but some things cannot be rushed.

The goal when feeding your baby is not to get all of the milk you have in the bottle into your baby – that would be a schoolboy error for this is not a yard of ale or some student drinking game.

The aim is simply to get as much of the milk in as your baby wants, without him coughing it all back up and rendering everything you've just done a complete waste of time. This simple step-by-step should hopefully help:

Step 1. If you're going to do this properly, go topless. Babies really dig skin on skin – it makes him feel like he's bonding properly and you feel strangely primeval.

Step 2. Hold your chosen arm at a ninety-degree angle and make a comfortable cradle for your baby to sit in. (Because this isn't a quick process, laying a small blanket over the arm before you plonk your baby in place may be wise.) Sitting him in an upright-ish position with his head and neck supported will help him breathe and swallow comfortably. But here's a crucial word of warning: never ever, ever prop the bottle and go off to do something else – even if you're really busy or you want a sandwich. Aside from being lazy and avoiding the close-contact bonding a baby needs, this increases the risk of your baby choking while you're not around.

Step 3. Place the teat gently on your baby's bottom lip and you should have ignition – if he doesn't lock on and begin guzzling straight away, squeezing a drop of milk onto his lip should kick-start things.

Step 4. Keep the bottle held at a gentle angle, whereby the formula fills the teat completely. If you allow air in, it will inflate your baby and what goes in will inevitably have to come back out in the form of small burps or, in really bad cases, a tsunami of milky vomit. Tilt the bottle slowly, at a pace your baby looks happy with – a newborn drinks slowly to begin with, speeding up as he gets bigger. If your baby starts to cough and splutter or has milk running out of the corner of his mouth, you've gone too fast or your bottle is jiggered and should be replaced. If at any point the teat becomes flattened, pull gently on the corner of your baby's mouth to release the vacuum. If the teat becomes blocked, apologise for the short delay as you replace it with another, which has to have been sterilized.

Step 5. Throughout feeding, maintain as much eye contact as possible and compliment your baby on how well he's doing. Tell him how clever he is and how well he's drinking this delicious milk, even though he won't understand a word of it and it may not even be true. Experts claim this praise can help create a tighter bond with your baby. No baby has ever been able to confirm this theory, but it's a nice idea.

Step 6. If you're feeding for some time, as is highly likely, you may need to swap arms after a while. This will not only bring feeling back to your 'support' arm but also give your baby a different view of the room and keep him more stimulated.

Step 7. It's oddly rewarding and entirely necessary to burp (aka 'wind') your baby frequently (see page 122) to expel any trapped air from his innards. You can also do it any time if he seems fidgety and uncomfortable during feeding.

Step 8. You're finished when your baby tells you he's finished, usually by pulling away from the teat. Burp him once again for good measure, wipe his mouth clean and pray he doesn't sick it all back up right at the end. If that happens you'll need to clean up the mess and start again because your baby's stomach will be empty. On those occasions it's OK to blaspheme, but do it quietly and under your breath.

Step 9. If, when you are finally finished, your baby is fast asleep, which is highly likely, then return him to his cot and congratulate yourself on a job well done. If he's wide awake and looks like he wants entertainment, take this opportunity to interact and bond. Introduce a small cuddly toy to the equation and intersperse your chat with the sort of goo-goo baby talk that would have you rolling your eyes if he wasn't your baby. Avoid overexciting him though, otherwise you may see that milk again.

Step 10. At the earliest opportunity, take the bottle apart fully and rinse the components, ahead of a proper soapy hot wash in the sink or dishwasher. Never save any milk that was left over for a later feed – the bacteria can run wild even if the milk is refrigerated.

Step 11. And of course if you haven't done so already, put your top back on.

Winding A Baby

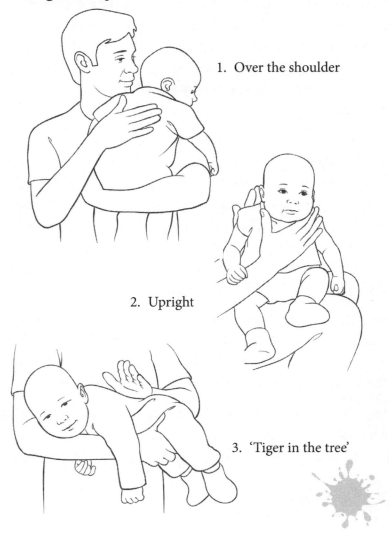

1. Over the shoulder

2. Upright

3. 'Tiger in the tree'

For simple people like me, winding is brilliant. Essentially, it's a game of cunning; attempting to coax out a large pocket of air from your baby by rubbing his back until it splurts out of his mouth with the type of belch you wouldn't be allowed to get away with. With babies it's different though. Even prim and proper people find it funny.

To prep for a burp, stick a muslin square or an old towel over your shoulder, then put your baby over it, supporting his head, and gently rub his back in a clockwise direction, applying firm but gentle pressure with the palm of your hand (1). You can also do this on your lap, with your baby sitting, leaning forwards while you support his head (2). Or try the 'tiger in the tree' position: lie the baby, belly down, along your arm and pat his back (3).

There is no right or wrong way to go about this – as long as your baby's comfortable and his neck and head are supported, your technique is probably right. Rub until he elicits a belch and probably a small pocket of milky vomit – known in this game as a posset, aka a puddle of regurgitated, curdled milk. This was the reason you stuck down a muslin square or towel at the start.

If your baby refuses to burp after five minutes' gentle coaxing, it may be that he has no wind to expel, which suggests you fed him very well indeed. If he doesn't appear to be uncomfortable, consider your work here done.

Posset Or Puke?

All babies will vomit in the first twelve months, so much so that you'd worry more if yours didn't. In the early weeks, this can be a natural reaction as his body adjusts to his new diet, while often you'll accidentally overfill him during feeding and he'll need to cough some of it back up.

If this happens, and what comes back up is a small splash of milk with a burp rather than a full tsunami, you have just witnessed a posset, which is a word and reaction you'll only encounter when you have a small baby.

The posset is simply a little pocket of regurgitated milk coughed up, most likely to occur in the first hour after feeding, and more likely to happen if your baby is being particularly active. A proper good burping helps minimize the chances of it happening. But when it does, just wipe it away and reassure your baby that everything's all right, because it usually is.

Note: *While a little posseting is nothing to be worried about, a lot of posset is more likely to be 'reflux'. If this is a regular occurrence and your baby appears to be in any kind of pain, talk to your doctor or health visitor.*

ESSENTIAL KIT

For bottle feeding a newborn baby, industry standard suggests you have about six 250 ml or 8 fl oz bottles. Bottles come in various shapes, all designed to eliminate air pockets and offering the most natural feeding ever created.

The teats also come in various shapes, made from various materials and with different hole sizes – smaller for younger babies who drink slowly and need a slower flow of milk, bigger for more advanced babies. Silicone teats were found to be the preferred choice in rigorous tests as they taste and smell of nothing, they don't get gummy, are dishwasher safe and are transparent, so you can be sure they're clean. But having said all of that, the truth is that trial and error is the best approach here until you hit upon the combination that works best for your baby.

BREAST MILK vs FORMULA MILK

Perhaps the greatest of the many dilemmas in a new parent's life is what to feed the baby in those early days. It's a straight choice between breast milk made quite literally in-house, or a strange powdery scientific substance sold in a carton or a can.

The problem, as you'll no doubt be aware, is that not every mum can breastfeed, even if she desperately wants to, as almost every responsible mother does. Your role here is simply to understand the situation, nod in all the right places and offer informed support if required.

Your response will need to go one of two ways:

1. If your baby's mum opts to breastfeed and has no problem on the production front, you need do nothing more than congratulate her on providing your baby with a mix of all the protein, fats, carbohydrates, vitamins, minerals, assorted nutrients and antibodies that help protect a newborn against illness and that can only be found in mother's milk. You will both smugly know that you are giving your baby the very best start in life, based on what loads of boffins have said down the years. However, you don't need to actually say anything, because you'll both already know all of the above.

2. However, if your baby's mum can't or won't be breastfeeding, this next bit is worth memorizing, particularly if she really wanted to. While breast milk is all well and good, formula milk is an excellent source of all the nutrients a baby needs to grow. Formula takes longer to digest and keeps a baby fuller for longer than breast milk, so your partner won't permanently have a baby clamped to her bosom. If she's tried to breastfeed, however briefly, but for whatever reason it didn't prove workable, you can remind her that even a single drop of breast milk will be of nutritional benefit. Most new mums who can't breastfeed will feel like they've in some way failed. Your job here is to convince them otherwise, without ever mentioning the F-word. It's all about putting a positive spin on it, so mention that breastfeeding doesn't fit in around work, which is important if she chooses to go back early. Formula feeding is helpful because even a doofus dad with sausage fingers can do the honours.

3. Also, mention that formula feeding means she's free to wear what she wants again, unfettered by a need to don a tent with easy-access boob flaps stitched in. And free to eat as she chooses again. Rather than having to eat loads of green stalks just to supercharge your new baby, now she can gorge herself on garlic and blue cheese and booze. Not all at the same time of course, although she could if she wanted to.

DADVICE Breast Is Not Always Best

In the months leading up to the birth of our boy, Jacob, we'd heard repeatedly that 'breast is best'. And it no doubt is, but two days in and Jacob was struggling to latch on. And even when he did, we couldn't tell if he'd taken any milk down. The fact he'd been surprisingly placid since we'd brought him home made us think we had the best behaved baby in the world. In reality, he wasn't getting enough food, so he just didn't have the energy to kick up a fuss.

On the third day, a health visitor came to help. All she could offer was to suggest Jacob's mouth was too small. We took offence and asked her to leave, then I went out and bought a pack of formula.

We watched in amazement as Jacob gulped the lot down then promptly fell asleep. Later, we bought a breast pump and did our best to alternate the feeding between breast and formula, and it worked.

At that point we learnt that it's what suits you and your child best when it comes to bringing up children . . . it's not always textbook!

PAUL M, JACOB AND MOLLY'S DAD

WEANING

*Breaking down the tricky transition from
liquids to solids . . .*

The move from milk to mushy food and on to proper solids takes
place in most babies around six months and is a very rewarding but
massively messy time. With that in mind, buy some bibs.

In those first six months your baby probably needs no solids
whatsoever, just milk from the breast or a big tin can. You can
introduce solids after four months if she seems ready (see page 129)
but only after checking with your doctor or health visitor first.

Now, the trick with solids is not to attempt to go from standing
to a full sprint in one session. You'll need to progress very slowly, bit
by bit, making small, baby steps. Your baby cannot go from drinking
milk on Monday to gnawing on a T-bone by Tuesday. You need to
build up slowly, gradually, until she's happy to up the volume and
variation.

But we're getting ahead of ourselves. First, we need answers to a
few questions I've taken the liberty of posing on your behalf . . .

Q. *When will I know my baby is ready to progress from milk to solids?*

A. That's an excellent question. There are typically five common signs to look out for:

1. She can sit up and hold her head steady.

2. She is showing an interest in your food.

3. She's mastered hand–eye co-ordination, so can look at her food, pick it up and put it in her mouth, unassisted. (The problem here is you'll only find that out for sure if you offer her some solid food, although many babies will show they can do it by eating crayons and the like.)

4. She can swallow food and attempts to do so if you offer her a tiny amount of purée on the end of your (clean) finger.

5. She still appears to be hungry even if you've increased milk feeds in an attempt to keep up.

Q. *When my baby is ready, how does this magical transition take place?*

A. Gradually and at your baby's speed is the first thing to reiterate. Be aware that how much she eats is far less important than your baby getting used to eating solid food. A safe first-step bet will be to start her off on mush – i.e. mashed or puréed food, or sugar-free cereal mixed with milk. This is not 'solid' in the classic sense, but it qualifies as a step in the right direction.

Good foods to mash or purée include soft fruits such as banana and apple, or potato and carrots – trial and error comes in here, but avoid anything that's overly sweet. If you get your baby hooked on sugar, even if it's natural, she won't ever eat anything else. Peel and wash all fruit and veg before puréeing and keep the flavours simple – mixing flavours like Daddy Wonka will confuse her very simple taste buds.

When she seems to have mastered mush, and is eating more than she's wearing, you can move up to the next-step foodstuffs. These include chicken, pasta, bread, toast, beans, rice, noodles and fish, making sure with forensic certainty that it contains no bones.

Avoid anything overly fatty or salty, and if you have the time and energy, feed home-made food rather than the stuff they sell in jars and sachets in the supermarket. These are usually bland, unhealthy and heavier on the salt and sugar than the food you can cook up at home. It's cheaper and better to cook in-house and freeze it in batches, ideally in labelled containers so you know what's what. The jarred stuff is best left for absolute emergencies.

Of course, if you're a responsible dad – and I doubt you'd have reached page 130 of this book if you weren't – then you'll be aiming to give your baby a balanced diet, mixing vegetables with meat or fish, some pulses, plenty of fruit and so on and so forth.

This is bad news in a sense because babies like to see their parents lead by example, so you'll need to start eating vegetables and pulses again and put the instant noodles and kebab meat on hold for a while.

By around a year, or as long as it takes at their pace, your baby will progress to having three meals a day. She can also be snacking on perennial baby classics such as carrot sticks, bread sticks and rice cakes. She'll drink less milk as a result and may even have dropped a feed, and this is good.

Banned Substances

While it's good to suggest what types of solid food your baby could be eating round about now, it's far more important to say here what not to give her. The following foodstuffs can cause allergies or make a baby sick: nuts of any kind, eggs, cow's milk (only safe from a year on), soft or unpasteurized cheese, shellfish, and liver, though that last one is surely a given.

ESSENTIAL KIT
A SEAT AT THE TABLE

Before your baby shows the first signs of wanting to progress from liquid to solids, you'll need to start thinking about advanced forms of baby seats specifically designed for feeding. You will need a high chair, preferably a decent one which features adjustable height settings and a removable baby table for when your baby wants to have her plate on the big table with you. Later, you might find a booster seat helpful – essentially a fairly cheap moulded plastic seat that straps securely onto your regular kitchen chairs and elevates your baby closer to the action.

Ten Important Rules About Feeding

1. Expect feeding to take longer and involve far more mess – all down your baby and you, and up your walls. Buy bibs and put any decorating on hold.

2. Start small and gradually increase. A blob of mush here, a teaspoon there – progress will take time. Use a plastic spoon, never metal as that will hurt your baby's gums.

3. If the food is hot, make damn sure it's not molten. By all means cook it to a very high and safe temperature, but let it cool to warm before serving, and always test it yourself.

4. Make sure your baby is sitting up straight throughout, to reduce the risk of choking, and never ever leave her alone while she's eating.

5. If your baby wants to feed herself, go with it and praise her for her sense of adventure. Buy more baby wipes.

6. If you're feeding with a spoon, wait until she opens her mouth before you offer it. Never attempt to shovel it in if she's not ready.

7. And if feeding with a spoon, avoid doing all that choo-choo train into the tunnel business – it's good fun to begin with but when your baby won't feed until you've taken the train thrice round the track, you've made life unnecessarily tough for future feeds.

8. If your baby wants to hold the spoon herself, that can only help. But again, never ever leave her alone while she's eating – you know the threat of choking hazards.

9. When she refuses food, she's more than likely finished. Expect smaller but more frequent meals while she makes the transition to solids.

10. If your baby's not ready, don't force-feed her. Just try again tomorrow.

DADVICE   Nothing Lasts For Ever

Just keep telling yourself that it's all just a phase. He's sleeping through the night, it's just a phase. My wife is going mad, it's just a phase. He's teething and it's terrible and he never stops crying, it's just a phase. I haven't slept in weeks, it's just a phase. He is so perfect, it's all going so well, it's just a phase. He's never sleeping and we're going crazy, it's just a phase. He won't eat, it's just a phase. He eats too much, it's just a phase. You'll get used to it.

DAVE A, FINN'S DAD

THE OUT-AND-ABOUT BABY BAG

*The precise art of packing a baby bag when
venturing out . . .*

In the past, before you were a parent, whenever you wanted to go out anywhere for the day, you just went. As long as you were wearing a pair of trousers you were pretty much set. Now you are a parent, all the rules have changed.

Every time you plan to go anywhere, even if it's for half an hour, it will need to be pre-planned with the precision of military manoeuvres or as if you were heading to the moon.

Nothing can be left to chance, which is why packing the out-and-about bag is traditionally a mother's job. Not because I am a tired old chauvinist, but because if it was left up to a dad to pack, it would contain a single nappy, half a bag of wipes, a dummy, and some biscuits. So, for future reference, just in case you are ever asked to pack your baby's bag, the following items should be considered the bare minimum. And do bear in mind that the longer you're out the more you'll need.

ESSENTIAL KIT
THE OUT-AND-ABOUT BAG

Nappies Pack what seems sensible for the length of time you'll be out, plus add at least two more to cover any disasters

A baby changing mat The light, rolled-up, transportable type, for impromptu changes

Baby wipes Never any less than half a packet, preferably a full one

A change of clothes and a hat And gloves if it's really cold out

Bottle(s) Made up, with the correct milk. Or bottle(s) and sealed carton(s)

Food + bowl + spoon(s) + bib(s) If you've moved up to solids

Dummies If you've embraced the dark side, and always more than one

A fluffy little toy With shaky bits. And maybe a baby book or two

Antibacterial hand sanitizer Because germs go out and about too

Paracetamol-based 'infant suspension' For any unexpected temperature issues

Tissues For any tissue issues

Suncream For when it's sunny out. Choose one suitable for babies – factor 50 should be sufficient protection

WASTE MANAGEMENT

*You are now in the waste management
business, and business is booming . . .*

You may pull the equality card and say changing a baby's bum is a job that should be shared equally between the parents. And you might be right. But I'd respectfully suggest you're wrong.

Given that you haven't spent the last nine months carrying your baby around inside you, while entirely sober, and given that you cannot breastfeed now your baby is out in the world, and given that you are not in pain after giving birth, then it makes sense that you should take control of this key area.

Particularly if your baby's mum is mainly breastfeeding, because taking control of waste management gives you a very easy way of bonding with your baby. And you're eighty per cent trained up already because wiping your baby's bottom isn't all that different to wiping your own.

But you still have that twenty per cent to learn. So, if you're signed up and prepared to get your hands dirty, let's start at the start . . .

The very first poo your baby produces will be unlike any other you've ever witnessed. The Magnificent Meconium Poo should arrive within about twelve hours of your baby's birth and will be impossible to miss – it will be a curious shade of blacky-green and superbly sticky, like the poo of a hungover Goth.

Once the first has arrived, the normal poos should arrive thick and fast, and often wet and fast as well, in all sorts of shapes, sizes and consistencies. For the first few weeks of your baby's life, you can expect him to go several times a day. How much should you expect? Well, that's a very good question.

Some babies produce so much poo, you'll wonder how something so small and delicate could have so much in him. Others can go days without passing so much as a pebble. Some babies are a combination of both – one minute producing enough wet poo to paint a shed, the next, barely a bean.

Either way, don't be too alarmed. All babies are different and if you're in any doubt about what is too much or too little, have a quiet word with your doctor or health visitor.

Which is all another way of saying: 'I can't tell you how much poo your baby should be doing, because nobody can say for sure.' What seems to be accepted as fact is that breastfed babies poo less often, and that poo production slows in all babies after the first few weeks.

What I can very happily advise you on though is how to react when faced with a nappy full of bottom waste. At the time of writing, I have 24,192 nappy changes to my name, and 24,191 of them can be considered a success, bar the one I accidentally smeared on the cream bedroom carpet in the middle of the night.

So, what I know about nappy changing is that it's a breeze, particularly if broken into a very simple step-by-step guide . . .

All Change

As mentioned earlier, your baby will need his nappy changed after he's had a feed, before he has a sleep and if he's crying because he's filled his nappy to the brim and doesn't like the feeling of sitting in his own slurry. And let's be honest, who does? Note also that newborns are said to urinate every twenty minutes, which goes down to once an hour by the time they're six months old. While his wee should be clear or pale, making it hard to distinguish, you'll know it's there by the weight of the nappy. Wet nappies should be changed quickly to avoid nappy rash.

The Nappy Change

Before you begin, find a flat, sturdy, safe surface – a changing mat on the carpet works very well, providing you have the flexibility required to get down and back up. If you're going to change on a high surface, remember to keep one hand on your baby's tummy at all times, otherwise he may roll or wriggle off the changing station and fall to the floor, and that isn't a risk worth taking. Once ready, the actual nappy changing should literally unfold as follows:

Step 1. With your baby on his back, place the spare nappy underneath his bottom. (This is good practice, having the new nappy close to hand, but it's also means that if, when you remove the spent nappy, your baby suddenly and without warning 'backfires', that spare will at least absorb some of the blow. Another wise manoeuvre when changing boy babies is to place a piece of tissue over his widdler, just in case he decides to water you. This is a common problem and an eye full of baby piddle will sting.

To speed up the changing process and reduce fiddling around, make sure the replacement nappy is the right way round, with the sticky tabs at the back and the happy animal face (or similar) at the front.

Step 2. Carefully undo the soiled nappy. You might recoil at its pungent innards the first time you change one, but you'll soon get used to it. Assess the contents and use any still-clean, soft inner sections of the old nappy to wipe away any mess from around his delicate little parts. Gently, grab both ankles and hoist your baby's bottom into the air, just high enough to whip the old nappy out from under him.

Step 3. Now, dip a cotton-wool ball in a bowl of warm water and wipe clean 'around the back', taking care to get into any baby creases. If your son is actually a daughter, it's important to say again that you should only ever wipe her front to back and never ever back to front, otherwise you risk spreading bacteria that can cause urinary-tract infections. While you're there, check for any nappy rashes that could later cause discomfort – the skin will be red and irate. Apply a nappy-rash cream if required.

Step 4. Lower him back onto that replacement nappy, pulling the front section through his legs and onto his tummy. Bring the side bits to the front and attach with the sticky tabs. Make sure it's snug but not overly tight, and if the umbilical stump is still there, fold down the top of the nappy so that it's outside the nappy. When all's good, dispose of the

old nappy in the bin. If your baby is still on a changing mat on top of a work surface and you wandered off to the bin to dispose of the nappy, he might now be wriggling off towards the painful fall we spoke of at the start. Run back as fast as possible to avert any danger and pay closer attention from now on.

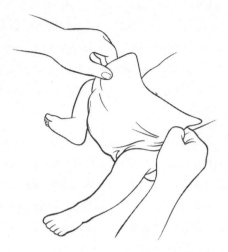

Step 5. Re-dress your baby, congratulate yourself on a job well disposed of, and try to blank from your mind that you have around 2,687 more to do over the course of the next year. Wash your hands a few times and prepare to change the next nappy in about five minutes.

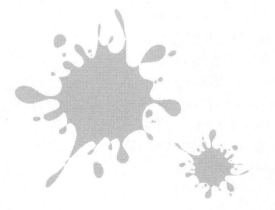

The Poo Chart

The colour, whiff and consistency of a baby's poo can change from day to day and week to week, particularly in breastfed babies – usually as a result of the mum's diet changing. Even so, just as an old crone can foretell the future through 'reading' tea leaves, it's possible to read the well-being of your baby by studying the shade and consistency of his deposit. To be honest, these are words I never expected to be typing. Even so, consider this a very rough guide to what's right and healthy and what may require further attention . . .

Yellowy-green

Usually the faeces of a healthy breastfed baby. Providing it has a runny consistency, a bit like diarrhoea, and very little odour, there should be nothing to worry about.

Light brown

Looks like peanut butter? Good. This is the stool of a healthy, formula-fed baby. Tastes like peanut butter too? Interesting. It should be fairly loose and may carry more of a whiff about it, but you can hardly complain, given the stench of some of yours.

Dark brown

The likely shade once your baby progresses to solid foods. The poo will have the mushy and loose consistency of peanut butter but come in a darker tone. Like if they mixed peanut butter with a hazelnut spread and a dash of water. However, the food he's fed will influence his poo. For example, feed him a lot of carrot and expect a more orange hue.

Dark brown with dots of colour

No need to worry here. It's most likely chunks of food passing through your baby too quickly for him to be able to digest properly. Play Spot The Veg to amuse yourself, as long as no one else is watching.

Runny yellow, green or brown

The consistency of wet paint, more watery than solid, delivered in a violent splat that explodes up the back of your baby's nappy. Classic diarrhoea, particularly if your baby suddenly becomes more regular. Keep an eye on this and if it happens more than two or three times, or if it doesn't pass within a day or two, call the doctor. One rule of thumb has it that if a baby violently backfires six times in twenty-four hours, seek urgent medical advice. It could be an infection, or it could just be a reaction to something you've fed him, possibly the formula milk. However, if left ignored, diarrhoea can cause dehydration, so don't sit around studying the shade for too long.

Green

This can be the result of certain types of infant formula, causing the poo to turn a darker shade of green and become more paste-like. It can also be caused by a sensitivity to certain foods, the side effects of medication or a stomach bug. If it doesn't return to 'normal' within a couple of days, see the doctor.

Very pale

This can be a sign of jaundice, common in newborns but usually clearing up within a couple of weeks. Again, if it persists, press the speed dial button for the doctor's surgery.

CLOTH vs DISPOSABLE NAPPIES

The hardest part of changing a baby's backside might actually be the moral dilemma involved in deciding which of the two types of nappy to use.

Disposable nappies are as disposable as the name suggests. You use them once, throw them in the bin and reach for another one. Then repeat, then repeat, then repeat.

Cloth nappies are designed for parents who care about the planet and literally don't mind getting their hands dirty. After each use, and despite being filled with baby waste, each nappy is scraped clean and washed at a high temperature, to be used repeatedly.

This sounds like no dilemma at all, until you factor in that over the course of your baby's first two and half years, it could cost you as much as £750 for all the disposable nappies you'll need, but just £350 for cloth.

Add in the fact that disposables are said to take 200 years to decompose and so sit festering on landfills, and you might suddenly feel some duty towards protecting the planet on which your new baby has just arrived. But it depends how hard you want to make things. Do you really have time to scrape baby poo from the inside of a nappy? Only you can decide.

Brown with red

The sight of poo dotted with blood will be alarming, but it can often be caused by tiny cracks in the skin around the bottom. This can often happen when their delicate little derrières attempt to pass hard poos. Apply nappy-rash cream but at the risk of sounding like a broken record (younger dads: ask your granddad what a record was), if it persists or the spots become streaks, call the doctor.

Rabbit droppings

Small and dry poos, or large, bulky boulders, passed sporadically and with your baby having to strain and cry in the process – this sounds like a painful case of constipation. Place a hand expertly on your baby's tummy and feel if it's tight – that's a telltale sign of constipation. It's more common in formula-fed babies, particularly if you get the quantities wrong and put too much powder in the water. Some parents suggest massaging your baby's stomach can help, while others recommend prune juice mixed with water or breast milk. However, because constipation can also be caused by a fever, dehydration, a change in diet or a reaction to a medication, if in any doubt, the doctor will be the best source of advice.

Nappy Changing

You will need more nappies than it bears thinking about. If you aim for a fairly average eight nappies a day, then times that by seven, you get fifty-six nappies a week. So, $56 \times 4 = 224$ a month, and $224 \times 12 =$ by crikey, you're suddenly looking at 2,688 nappies in a single year, and that's a fairly conservative guesstimate. Obviously you don't need them all from the off, but you will need a big pile to get you through the first few days. And even if using reusable nappies, you'll need some disposables as well, just in case.

But that's not all. You'll also need nappy bags, because where are you going to put all those soiled nappies? Buy one hundred nappy bags from the pound shop, or 300 dangerously thin bags from the 50p shop. And because your backside would be chaffed too if you were getting through 56 nappies and a million bum wipes a week, you'll also need nappy-rash cream, which offers blessed relief from the very common sore bum syndrome.

Finally, you'll need a nappy changing 'station', on which you will perform your nappy changing duties. Should you opt for a handsome, hand-crafted mahogany cabinet with superb storage space for nappies and creams; a glorified cake trolley on wheels; or a cheap oblong of plastic-covered foam that sits on the floor?

I'd suggest the latter, based on experience, because it's cheap, easy to store out of sight and because a wriggling baby falling half a centimetre off a mat on the floor will do himself far less damage than a baby falling five feet off an ergonomically impressive mahogany changing station. But it's all about opinions in this game and really, only you can decide.

DADVICE Ignore Most Advice

The most difficult part of the first twelve months was the major adjustment we had to make. Parenting classes gave us pointers on caring for a newborn baby but nothing can prepare you for the whirlwind of the first twelve months.

The key lesson I learnt, what we both learnt, was that as long as your child is healthy and thriving, there is no right or wrong way of caring for them. What might work for 'textbook' children may not work for yours. Go with your instincts, even from the early days. Expert guidelines and information are important but you know your baby better than a midwife or health visitor because you are with them twenty-four hours of the day. You know how they react and behave, what they do and don't like, what is right and what is wrong.

I'd say the key is to make the baby's home as stress-free as possible. Stressed parents make for a stressed baby which results in a turbulent home environment, which is not good when you're tired and confused and just trying your very best to do what's right.

BEN H, EVA AND ISSY'S DAD

SAFETY-PROOFING

*Danger lurks around every corner for the
intrepid and adventurous baby . . .*

Until your baby learns to crawl and clamber around independently,
your house shouldn't present any real danger to her safety or well-
being. Before six months she will mainly stay where you leave her,
which is a good thing.

However, as soon as she is mobile and can pull and yank at things,
every single thing in your home becomes a potential threat to her
safety and everything will need to be baby-proofed.

This means your stairs will need stair gates top and bottom, or
you'll need to move into a bungalow. Any dangerous corners on
fixtures, fittings or furniture will need fat rubber plugs attaching in
case your baby should fall into them and split something soft open.

Every door will need a funny sponge door stopper, to prevent it
closing fully and trapping fingers. The fire will need a metal guard,

or to be never ever turned on for fear she will burn herself to a crisp on it. Scalding hot cups of tea will need to be kept well out of her grabbing reach. Your cupboard full of cleaning products and industrial poisons will need a kiddie lock on it. And all the plug sockets will need plastic socket covers to stop your baby shoving her fingers in and filling herself full of volts.

More important than any product you can buy, however, is the new mindset you'll need as a result of your baby becoming more upwardly mobile. Now she is learning to move and has become obsessed with exploring every last corner of every room she enters, you need to grow eyes in the back of your head and be on a permanent state of high alert. From this point on you'll need to think ten steps ahead and assess the threat of danger in every room you enter, scanning for anything that could fall, topple or drop onto your baby's head. There's obviously much to admire in the sight of her fearlessly scaling the bookcase for the first time, but not if it topples over on her. Being squashed to death by a pile of Harry Potters is no way to go.

Accidents And Injuries

Every house with a newborn baby needs a first-aid box packed full of essential emergency products, should any low-level, this-doesn't-need-qualified-medical-assistance accident occur. And it inevitably will.

Having a proper box (with a stout fastening mechanism) serves two key purposes. It keeps all the things you need together in one place so you know exactly where they are when needed. And it makes you feel a bit like a qualified doctor.

Anyway, make sure your special medical box is big enough to hold at least the following goods:

ESSENTIAL KIT
THE SOS BOX

Plasters Lots of small ones, for a smaller-shaped person

Bandages and adhesive tape, should it escalate from simple plasters

Antiseptic wipes and cream to clean cuts and grazes and help prevent infection

Nappy-rash cream for blessed relief

Paracetamol, aka infant suspension – a quick-fix for soaring temperatures

Spoon, dropper or syringe for the swift and clean administering of medicinal drops

Dioralyte (one suitable for babies) for rehydrating a dehydrated baby fast

A digital thermometer for taking an accurate temperature, either in the ear or under the arm

Calamine lotion for itchy rashes

WARNING!

Fear Everything

While it's true that a baby who can crawl and clamber becomes a very real danger to herself, the threat can begin earlier – from the point yours first begins to wriggle and roll. It's all too easy to take your eye off her while she appears to be safely lying on your bed in the bright spring sunshine. The birds are chirping and you decide to answer the call of nature. You will only be twenty seconds if you work fast, you tell yourself, but no sooner have you left the room than you hear a heavy, horrible thud. That will be the sound of a baby falling off the bed. And it happened. Twice. In the space of a week, once on my watch, once on my wife's. I don't think it made us bad parents. We just switched off and let our guard down a bit, and then spent the next three weeks fearing a knock on the door from The Authorities. Let's not point the finger though. Let's just agree that as soon as your baby is capable of any sort of movement in any direction, you'll need to train your brain to fear anything and everything.

DADVICE Just Be On Call

The one thing that caught me off guard was the feeling of being lost and useless. I was more like a sleep-deprived butler than a dad in those early days. In all honesty, you don't need to be there for the baby, you just need to be there to do what you're needed to do and help keep your partner sane. It's crucial that you make sure your partner is as happy as possible. A happy mum is a better mum and that makes for a happy and better dad. It will be tough and tiring, of course it will, but just roll with the punches because it really does get easier.

The best advice I can offer would be to try to eat properly. We had no family around to help us so we ended up trying to save time by eating quick food, but quick food is usually unhealthy and it makes you feel rubbish. Try to batch-cook healthy meals when you get a chance – it will save you time when you've had a rough night.

MAL B, LILY-SUN'S DAD

WARNING!
Head Banger

If your baby accidentally takes any kind of bang or blow to her head but there are no outward signs of any kind of damage, bar perhaps a bump or a mark, apply a cold compress – i.e. a cold, damp cloth or a bag of garden peas from the freezer, wrapped in a tea towel – and assess the situation for the next twenty-four hours. If she loses consciousness, becomes drowsy and can't be easily woken, starts to vomit, seems disorientated or anything worse, call an ambulance with great haste. If she seems otherwise fine but you're mildly concerned it needs to be checked out, see a doctor or head to the hospital.

PART THREE

THE IMMEDIATE PANIC IS OVER, WHAT'S NEXT?

TAKING CARE OF BUSINESS PART I

*The stuff you're legally obliged to do as the
parent of a new baby . . .*

It's rarely mentioned that when you have a baby you are required to fill out loads of pesky paperwork. Your baby is a bit like a washing machine in that sense – unless you send the insurance documents back to the manufacturer, you're not fully covered, and so it sort of is with your baby.

To make him official in the eyes of the law, there are two key things you will need to do within the first few weeks. Check the details with your health visitor, but they usually involve:

1. Registering the birth, to get your baby into The System and be issued with a birth certificate.

2.   Giving your baby a name, usually within a set number of days. Both are important, but the naming is deserving of a full entry of its own . . .

Name And Shame

When naming your baby, tread carefully and try hard to avoid saddling him with a name he'll grow up to despise you for. I say this because in recent years, every rule of taste and common sense that ever applied to naming a baby has been ripped up. Nowadays, it's a lawless free-for-all with practically no boundaries. Not like in The Old Days.

Take 1914, for example. A century ago the most popular baby names for a boy and girl in Britain were John and Mary. Fifty years later, it was David and Susan. And by 2012, when the most recent figures were available, Harry and Amelia had hit top spot.

Nowadays, a new spate of more creative baby branding has taken hold, inspired by Uncle Sam. In the US, in an attempt to prove that their baby is not just like every other baby, the names are becoming increasingly ~~insane~~ individual. A recent list in the US outlined some of the more creative names registered and included the likes of Ace, Jedi, Mowgli and, ironically, Sanity.

The UK top ten names are entirely sane by comparison, but give it five years and you can't help but wonder how high Gherkin, Google or Ga-Ga might have climbed up the British list.

Now I can't advise you on how to name your baby, it's absolutely none of my business and I'm no arbiter of taste – how could I be when my middle name is Lee? All I would say is that if you are pondering a suitable name for your tiny little baby, just ask yourself one question. If you were to wake up one morning and realize, for the first time in your life, that you'd been saddled with Heavenlee or J'Adore, Thunder or Jaxxon for the rest of your days, how would you feel?

Name In Haste...

In various other countries where they take naming their babies very seriously indeed, there is a long list of names that have been banned for being just too out there and/ or irresponsible. The authorities in New Zealand in particular keep a very tight check on things and have in recent years outlawed the likes of Lucifer, Justus, * [star symbol] and Talula Does The Hula From Hawaii – the latter belonged to a nine-year-old girl who pronounced it 'K' so as to avoid being humiliated at school. In Britain, however, there are no such rules and you can call your baby whatever you please. Luckily, and no doubt with that in mind, it's possible to get the birth certificate changed within the first year if you do make a terrible mistake – and in the US, name-change remorse is also on the rise. After that first year, changing it becomes a more complicated and costly business.

DADVICE Learn Fast

The hardest thing about becoming a new dad is the huge change that happens virtually overnight. While your partner is going through nine months of pregnancy, your daily routine doesn't really change. When Ruby was born, the first two to three weeks were relatively easy, as it was all new and you'd be at home. The really hard work started when you had to combine looking after a baby (and mother) with going to work – and going back to work is definitely the easier option.

I'm not sure there is a guaranteed, fail-safe way to prepare yourself. Just go with your gut instinct every time. You can spend your whole time taking advice off people, looking on the internet, following other people's schedules and so on, but you just have to go with your baby and go with your instinct because no one knows a baby better than the parents.

Also help each other out by catching up on rest, even if it's just for a couple of hours here or there. I spread my annual leave out – instead of taking two weeks off, I took ten Fridays off so that I had nearly three months of short weeks; that helped a lot.

MATT H, RUBY AND HARRY'S DAD

TAKING CARE OF BUSINESS PART II

*The stuff you're not legally obliged to do as
the parent of a new baby but may still want
to think about . . .*

Having a baby can help focus a man's mind on the important things
in life. Things you never really considered – or wanted to consider –
before you had a baby suddenly become of paramount importance. I
would suggest you add the following to your To Do list:

1. Start Saving

As mentioned earlier on, running a small baby up to adulthood could
well push you to the brink of financial oblivion, unless you take great
care of your funds. Your days of decadent excess may have to be put
on hold for a while and your belt slightly tightened.

2. Set Up A Bank Account

You will already have one, I assume, so this is for your baby. The rate of interest may be pitiful and the risk of banks closing down and losing all of your money has never been higher, but an account for your baby is an obvious but responsible option. For the full range of options speak to your bank, but the point is it's never too soon to start saving.

3. Make A Will

I didn't want to be the one to break this to you, but one day you will die. Not for a while, we hope, but eventually and inevitably and hopefully with great dignity and all that. When that day comes, to make sure all your worldly possessions go to the right people/person, you'll need to finally get round to drawing up that will you've been putting off for years because it's all so depressing. But now is the time and you can draft one yourself using a self-starter pack available on the high street, or pay a solicitor to take care of it for you. As before, do your homework on the best options open to you and leave no stone unturned.

4. Take Out Life Insurance

If you don't already have life insurance, there's nothing like a baby arriving to make you start thinking you should probably have some. Nobody's out to get you, that I know of at least, but none of us can predict what's lurking around the corner and we owe it to our offspring to have every eventuality covered.

5. Get A Passport

Now this isn't quite so gloomy but it's every bit as pressing if you plan to take your baby abroad for a bit of culture or some sun, or both. Even tiny babies need their own passports, ridiculously, which means yours will need a mug shot taking, even though in a matter of months she won't look anything like she does in this shot. But this is not optional and it means you'll need to take your baby to one of those photo booths and ask her to sit still and smile at the camera while you try to keep your hands and arms out of shot.

My wife and I tried this with our two boys at six months old – and it quickly unravelled into a sorry farce. In the end, having spent all our cash failing dismally to get a shot that would legally pass muster, we took them to a local chemist that offered a more 'bespoke' photographic service – basically, they had a camera in the back and kept snapping until they got what we needed. This was ultimately a far cheaper and easier option, and one we wished we'd known about earlier.

DADVICE Count To Three (Then To Ten)

Being a dad for the first time is a brilliant experience but you will need the patience of a saint to come through it unscathed. Crying won't stop in seconds, nappies can overflow with excrement that goes up to your baby's neck, and your wife will be a little crazy at times. Teething in particular is a truly horrible time. I sang (then hummed as I backtracked out the bedroom door) 'Twinkle, Twinkle' hundreds of times trying to soothe my son back to sleep in the middle of the night. Learn where the creaky floorboards are in the nursery and avoid them at all costs. Just count to ten and soldier on. Things will improve at three months. And bear in mind that you'll make new friends and lose old ones. That's the way it goes. You'll be too busy to worry.

TIM S, HARRY AND ROBIN'S DAD

RETURNING TO WORK

A word of warning, because this can be
fraught with danger . . .

When returning to work after your paternity leave, you will re-enter your workplace looking very tired but very proud. However, once back at your desk you'll need to be aware of certain unwritten rules now that you are a parent.

Firstly, when a colleague asks how things have been, keep your response brief. Proud, but brief. Unless they have children of their own and are genuinely interested in comparing notes or reminiscing on how it was when they were in your position, while being silently thankful they're no longer going through it themselves, they are only being polite. They don't really want to know in exhaustive detail anything about the birth itself, the precise procedure required for serving milk at 3 a.m., or the legal requirements for registering your baby.

Just give them a concise, top-line response, making clear that it's tough and tiring but ultimately the greatest thing you've ever done or will ever do, and then let them get on with whatever it is they do for a living.

Also, crucially, try not to talk endlessly about how tired you are. People can see that for themselves by your dead eyes so they don't need to be constantly reminded, plus it just makes you sound ungrateful.

And a few months down the line, when your baby is picking up every illness under the sun and passing it on to you, try not to bleat too much about how ill you're feeling. Firstly, because you asked for all of this and you therefore have a duty to 'man up' and crack on. And also because if you're telling your colleagues about your latest illness, you're sharing more than just information with them.

But the biggest and most important lesson upon returning to work is that you should never forget that whatever line of work you are in, you have it easier than any mum still at home raising the baby. Mothers get time 'off work', which sounds brilliant for getting really good at *Call Of Duty*. But, every one of those days will be taken up with a screaming newborn baby who will test her patience and sanity.

So if, when you've returned to work, you come home and your partner asks how your day has been, it pays to heavily exaggerate your workload and paint every day as having been like doing a double shift breaking boulders in hell. Whatever you do, never let on that you've spent most of the day watching videos of dogs riding motorbikes on the internet and feeling slightly bored. Your other half would not take kindly to this, so engage the brain before you deliver a response.

CHILDCARE

Help is always at hand.
(All major credit cards accepted . . .)

Should you or your baby's mum not be aiming to raise your baby 24/7/365, you will no doubt need to investigate the childcare options available to you. Generally, you can expect it to come down to three main options:

1. A Childminder

You can pay a childminder to look after your baby for as many hours and days a week as you are both happy to commit to. This usually means dropping your baby off at the childminder's house whenever it suits, but be aware that a one-to-one arrangement is unlikely – he'll almost certainly have to share the minder's time and attention with one or two other babies.

2. A Nanny

You can pay a nanny to do much the same as a childminder, but generally a nanny will offer the one-to-one care you might prefer for your baby. Unlike a childminder, the nanny will usually come to your house, making transportation far less of an issue. They sometimes even live in your house if you have enough rooms and don't find it all a bit weird. With both options 1 and 2, recommendations from friends and fellow parents usually works best and gives you more peace of mind. However, with a decision this important, make sure the person you entrust to care for your baby has all the relevant badges, certificates and qualifications to do the job.

3. The Nursery

Perhaps the most common alternative to a stay-at-home parent, the nursery can come into play from as early as three months in and is a very simple deal. You pay a hefty price for trained staff to look after your baby during the day, freeing you and your partner to go back to work and earn the money that will end up paying for the nursery care.

Now you might feel guilty in the first few weeks, when you drop your tiny baby off at nursery and hand over the responsibility of bringing him up during daylight hours to a total stranger. But you'll soon notice that almost all the babies there are happy and have forgotten about their mum and dad before the parent has even exited the room. There almost certainly will be tears along the way, but in time, and quicker than you might think, the nursery will become like a second home to your baby.

It's important to stress that if you do opt for a nursery, make sure you research your options thoroughly, checking out official reports to find the best available to you. Just as importantly, make sure you act as early as possible, particularly if you live in an area where demand ridiculously outstrips supply. I speak from experience on this point. When our babies were still doing their nine-stretch inside their mum's tummy, my wife and I went to the local nursery for a look around and to sign on the dotted line. The place was quite nice, as it should be for the princely sum they were demanding. Only when we reached the end of the tour, the proprietor explained that we'd need to go on the waiting list as they had no space, so our twin boys were placed at numbers 238 and 239. A year later we received a call from the nursery asking if we still wanted the places, because they were now up to 187 and 188 and apparently moving fast up the list. By that point we had moved sixty miles away, partly to get into a nicer, less busy nursery, so we politely declined. The message here, then, is book early to avoid disappointment. And of course, prepare to be astounded by how much they charge.

DADVICE Jack In Your Job And Stay At Home

When I told my friends that I was giving up work, their reactions were full of references to daytime TV and yummy mummies. It wasn't until they had kids of their own that they started to understand the reality of it. Babies have no off buttons and an amazing appetite for the world around them. It's amazingly rewarding but undeniably exhausting.

Several things have helped me adjust to being a man in a woman's world. Groups were particularly helpful – having a social network and the chance to chat about grown-up stuff whilst the kids play is a good way to maintain your sanity. Fresh air is also essential – take a trip to the park, the library or a stroll with the scooter. Just getting out really makes a difference.

Perhaps most importantly, it helps to do 'man things'! Having a distraction from family life is essential. I go fishing but other men may go to the pub or play football. I've found it essential to re-charge my batteries every now and then.

Knowing what I know now, I'd say that you get out what you put in. The harder you try the more fun you'll have and the more your kids will love you for it.

CRAIG G, OLIVER AND JASMINE'S DAD

CROWD CONTROL

How to cope – and deal – with a steady
supply of well wishers . . .

During the first few days and weeks of parenthood, you might as well leave your front door on the latch. You'll be welcoming a steady stream of happy, smiling family and friends in your house, all of them keen to see your new addition and share in the warm glow of parenthood. (Be warned that for some reason, every woman who enters your house will desperately need to smell your baby's head. I still don't know why, but don't attempt to stop them having a good sniff.)

For the most part, taking in visitors will be a joyful time where your baby is the centre of attention and you can bask in the reflected glory. But, well, this only works if your visitors adhere to the rules.

The best visitors you can receive are those who bring with them food – a nice pie or a lasagna that you can heat up when they've gone to make life just a little bit easier. Or those who offer to take your baby out for a stroll for an hour while you have a wash and brush your teeth. And those who somehow instinctively know when it's time to go home without needing to be told.

The very worst visitors eat all your biscuits, drink all your tea and simply will not head off despite your woefully unsubtle hints.

You'll no doubt receive both types of visitor in the coming weeks, so it pays to have a plan for dealing swiftly with those who outstay their welcome. Establish a 'trigger phrase' with your partner – 'liquid meconium' would do – and when that phrase is spoken, you as the man of the house should be responsible for shepherding your guests to the door.

Be as polite as possible, but if Auntie Edna needs ejecting head first into the conifers, sometimes that's just how it has to play out. Because anybody who doesn't recognize that your time and tea bags are precious really has no place in your home.

DADVICE Buy More Tea Bags

There are so many things you probably won't be prepared for when you become a new dad. I certainly wasn't prepared for the overwhelming amount of love that you feel straight away – any fears or concerns just disappear once you have the baby in your arms. I also wasn't prepared for the onslaught of visitors and the amount of tea bags they'd get through either, so it's the little things as well as the big.

After spending all my life sleeping through the night, I wasn't prepared for suddenly having an in-built alarm that woke me at the slightest murmur. I wasn't prepared for the amount of baby stuff that brilliantly comes your way as hand-me-downs. And I certainly wasn't ready for having to go back to work after two weeks' paternity leave. It's gut-wrenching to have to leave, because you want to be with your baby all the time.

My advice? Take the full allocation of paternity leave, your new family needs you. Give your baby as many cuddles as you can, they don't stay little for long – and forget what it says in the books about putting the baby down at every opportunity and just enjoy being with them. Above all, throw yourself into the situation. It's a very steep learning curve, but you end up learning fast.

SIMON B, LAYLA AND ROSS'S DAD

SEX

*That's right, this is a short and awkward
chapter about doing 'it' . . .*

So, the big question. How soon is too soon to be doing 'it' again? Erm, well. Er. The thing is, I can't claim to be any kind of sexual guru. I can't even prove I've ever even done it, as my boys were the product of IVF. But I have. I definitely have.

Anyway, as you're still reading I can only assume you need some sort of help or guidance on this subject and don't have anyone else to turn to. So, all I would say is that you may need to downgrade your expectations in the days, weeks, even months following the birth of your first child. Your other half may beg to differ, but be prepared for sex to be less plentiful and certainly less athletic than it perhaps was before you became a dad.

The experts suggest No Sex For Six Weeks, and with good reason. Your partner may well be in a certain amount of discomfort, having effectively just passed the equivalent of a bowling ball through her cervix. Or she'll have had her stomach cut open if it was a 'sun roof'

C-section birth. Either way there will be stitches, tears and lacerations involved and the last thing she will want is you jumping around on top of her in nothing but your sports socks.

And of course, there is also the fact that she will be sleep deprived, on account of waking constantly through the night to feed your newborn baby, so working through every entry in the Karma Sutra probably won't be top of her list of priorities. Plus, having carried a large baby inside her for nine months, she may well have one or two 'body issues'. It's not uncommon for a new mum to feel unattractive after giving birth. Your job will be to shower her with compliments and reassurances, and not simply because you have ulterior motives in mind.

In time, I'd say that it's important you do rekindle your sex life to ensure you're a fully functioning couple, rather than just a mum and a dad – and because if you don't use your bits they might fall off. But give it a little time is the best unqualified advice I can offer here.

QUESTIONS AND ANSWERS

Your baby will soon be mistaking you for the cleverest man on earth . . .

In a couple of years' time, once your baby begins to talk and make sense of the world around her, she'll start to throw questions at you from every imaginable angle. Apparently, according to some recent research, the parents of a single small child have to answer, on average, 390 questions every single day – which clocks up at 105,120 questions a year.

Admittedly a lot of those questions will be 'Daddy whatiszis?', when you place a bowl of mysterious puréed mush on the table, and so will be easy to answer. But the other stuff will genuinely test your brainpower and recall of school subjects:

'Why is the sky blue?'

'What happened to the dinosaurs?'

'Why did Grandma die?'

Soon, you will need to be an expert in every single subject ever taught, answering each question with complete confidence and absolute accuracy. If you bluff your way through and make up what sounds about right, that answer will become Fact in your toddler's head, and she'll grow up thinking the moon really is made of Stilton.

Of course, this is not a real issue for now, because not even Einstein was asking existential questions in his first year, but now is the time to start reacquainting yourself with all the stuff you never paid attention to at school, college and university. History, quantum physics, the meaning of life and everything else. Because you owe it to your baby.

MIND YOUR LANGUAGE

*Advance warning: your baby can hear
everything . . .*

Another subject that falls into the 'Not For Now But You Should
Really Start Thinking About It' category is The Way You Speak. Not
so much the way you routinely butcher the basic rules of grammar,
although that will be picked up on and parroted, but more the string
of obscenities you may allow to float off your tongue. Until you
become the parent of a pure, untainted baby, your language can be
as coarse and hoary as the circles you move in allows. For most of us
adult males, 'fruity' and often near-the-knuckle language becomes
the norm in life. Bawdy chat and bad language are just what we do,
even if we're respectable types with no real reason to swear. It's just a
light dose of Tourette's, and although it doesn't reflect well, it doesn't
make you a bad man. But soon it might.

Research has shown that babies are listening to your conversation while they're in their mother's womb, so every swear word is being monitored by your progeny from the inside.

Initially, this won't matter because he doesn't understand what you're saying. But by seven months your baby should be able to respond to the sound of his own name and by the time he's a year old he'll recognize simple commands such as Yes and No.

Somewhere between twelve and twenty-four months, your baby may be able to talk in two- and three-word sentences, and by the age of three, he could well have mastered hundreds of words.

So, unless you're an irresponsible disgrace of a dad, you won't want any of those words to be anything you wouldn't say in front of a nun. Since you don't want your beautiful little baby to be parroting the obscenities he heard you scream when you stubbed your toe the other day, now is the time to act. It took a while to condition your brain into thinking that peppering an ordinary and affable conversation with F-bombs was reasonable, and it will take even longer to retrain your brain into filtering such obscenities out before they hit the airwaves.

Now is the time to start retraining your brain, ideally before the baby arrives but at the very latest, before he can understand what you're saying.

HOW TO BE A GOOD DAD

The sage advice of several good mothers.
It will pay to take heed . . .

Corner The Catering

I think the best thing your partner can do in those early days, weeks and months is anything relating to food and refreshments. Before he left for work in the mornings, Nick used to deliver Holly to me, accompanied by a cup of tea and some toast because he knew I was terrible at sorting my food out and probably wouldn't eat until he got home from work. This was a particular blessing on the days when I was struggling with breastfeeding and had switched mostly to formula, but was still managing a feed in the mornings, which took an absolute age. Nick sorting Holly and my breakfast out helped me go on a bit longer, until she was more interested in eating porridge for breakfast.

LYNN S, HOLLY'S MUM

Do Sweat The Small Stuff

As I fed our baby myself I think there were times in the early days where Simon probably felt a bit redundant. The small things he did made the biggest difference though, such as when Layla woke in the night for a feed, he would place a pillow under my arm, or take her and do the nappy change or make sure I had a glass of water. His constant reassurance that he was always there for us and telling me how proud he was of me made things all the better. I'd suggest that if there is something special that your partner can do with the baby then it helps with their bond – Simon would take Layla swimming every week since she was nine weeks old, meaning that until our second child was born, I could enjoy a very welcome lie-in!

MUNENI B, LAYLA AND ROSS'S MUM

Don't Poison Your Baby

My boyfriend really helped me by just being there and going through it all with me. Bringing cups of tea and doing the washing, keeping the house clean and looking after visitors were all his jobs and he did it very well. I know people say that you should just forget about the housework but living in a dirty, messy house would have really ruined the new fresh baby experience for me. It didn't all go to plan of course. There was an occasion where he accidentally ended up soaking nipple shields in neat Milton solution, so our baby ended up sucking on a small amount of neat bleach. Luckily, it didn't cause any harm and it was never repeated. Remembered, yes, but never repeated. More impressively, he excelled in doing the shopping. There was one particularly memorable supermarket list that consisted solely of maternity pads, breast pads, cotton wool and nappies. It was the lightest, bulkiest, most absorbent shop possible! He wasn't embarrassed and didn't complain – he just got on with it and got the job done!

LUCY C, MUM OF TWO

Just Be There

I remember being absolutely terrified of suddenly having responsibility for another human being; this tiny, delicate little baby. Twenty-four hours earlier I had never even held a newborn baby or changed a nappy. Paul just being there was a great comfort blanket for me. He was always very supportive and reassuring that we did know what we were doing, even when at times we didn't. He was also very hands-on from Day One, helping with nappy changing, feeding and middle of the night crying. Also, when he went back to work, he would come home at lunchtime to check on us. I very much appreciated this, as a four-hour stretch on my own was much less daunting than a full day and those little things can make a big difference.

TAMMY M, JACOB AND MOLLY'S MUM

Role Play

Nick was very useful when our twins were little, but he didn't have much choice as there were two to look after and it was all hands on deck. Very early on he decided that when we were both in the house, responsibilities would be split. As he put it, I was responsible for our sons' Food & Beverages and he was Waste Management. This worked very well, but waste management does of course come to an end, while food and beverages goes on for ever. He would also take responsibility for the late feed and entertainment, so I could skip off to bed around 8.30 p.m. and get some sleep before the 2 a.m. feeds. Looking back now, I was always very grateful to him for getting home from work promptly to lighten the load and at weekends he would look after them whilst I had some 'me time' at the supermarket (hey, life changes!). Basically, as long as you remember you are a team, you can't go far wrong.

SARAH H, LOUIS AND JIM'S MUM

Formulate A Plan

Going back to work was the key time as far as we were concerned and we had to formulate some kind of plan that made it workable. We quickly realized that Martha's night-time feeds had to be phased out and that we had to take control of the situation. The problem was that when she woke in the middle of the night, all she wanted from me was to be fed, so I had no chance of settling her back to sleep. Which meant that Chris had to be the one who got up in the night and sat in the dark, comforting her until she would finally go back to sleep – the happy by-product of that was that I got more sleep! It took a few weeks, but our quest for the Holy Grail was complete – Martha was sleeping through! Sometimes you have to force things a bit and make it work around your whole life.

CLAIRE V, MARTHA AND DAN'S MUM

Work Together

Initially, Matt made himself very useful by taking care of all the shopping, cooking and housework that needed to be done. That was a big worry off my mind and it left me to concentrate on learning how to be a mum, because it was as new to me as being a dad was to Matt. After a couple of weeks we'd established a bit of a feeding pattern where we'd work in shifts so that we both got some decent sleep during the night, which made life manageable. And the other really good thing was that he used to take Ruby out on a Saturday morning, meaning I had a day to have a lie-in and he had valuable bonding time and the chance to do his own thing. I think it's the little things like this that really help.

MEL H, RUBY AND HARRY'S MUM

THE NEXT TWELVE MONTHS AND BEYOND

A quick guide on what you can expect after the first year . . .

There are no guarantees of course, because all babies are different and – yes, you know the rest. However, it's not unrealistic to hope that your baby might be:

Talking Confidently: Between Twelve – Twenty-Four Months

Between the first and second year, your baby's vocabulary will begin to grow. And it will apparently need to, if reports from America are to be believed. According to the results of the American Association for the Advancement of Science, the average child should have mastered twenty-five words/phrases by twenty-four months. And those words, to tick off, are: Mummy, Daddy, baby, milk, juice, hello, ball, yes, no, dog, cat, nose, eye, banana, biscuit, car, hot, thank you, bath, shoe, hat, book, all gone, more and bye-bye.

Anything less than those twenty-five is apparently cause for concern, so your job is to help develop and expand your baby's vocabulary by reading that list to them every night before bed. Either that or just relax and don't get too hung up on it. Keep talking to your baby and everything will probably turn out just fine. By the age of three, those twenty-five words may have become several hundred.

Getting Up And Downstairs Unaided: Between Twelve – Twenty-Four Months

Probably closer to the two-year mark than the one, but scaling the stairs is usually accomplished with relative ease. Obviously, although they seem confident, it pays to keep a close eye at all times to avoid them making the downward journey face first. They should also be able to run and climb all over your sofa by the time they turn two, which is a good and a bad thing.

Becoming More Upwardly Mobile: Between Thirteen – Fifteen Months

The independent gene really starts to kick in around now. Babies will start to want to do more for themselves, which means feeding and trying to dress themselves, which means the food will end up down their chin and your walls and they'll wear their trousers or dress on their head. They may still be some way off being able to eat at the table using cutlery properly, however – this usually comes between the ages of two and three.

Constructing Sentences: Between Eighteen – Twenty-Four Months

They should be learning to throw or kick a ball and be starting to string two or three words together around now. You should be able to hold a proper conversation with your baby between the ages of three and four, when they are no longer a baby but have suddenly become a child without you realizing.

Potty Training: Between Eighteen Months – Four Years

This massive milestone will come no earlier than eighteen months, but could also be dragged out as far as their fourth birthday if they're really not ready. Don't rush them where bodily waste is concerned. If it backfires, you'll be left cleaning up.

Having Bad Dreams: Between Two – Three Years

If your baby is troubled by thoughts of monsters and beasties in the night, it'll most likely start between the ages of two and three when their imagination has been fired by stories, television and the little boys they hang around with who you think are probably a bad influence.

Riding A Bike And Moving Up To A Big Bed: Between Two - Three Years

Learning to ride a bike is another great milestone; some children can even balance without stabilizers between three and four years old. Also, they will probably be ready to move into a big bed of their own by around the age of three. And as their confidence continues to climb, expect bigger, louder, trickier tantrums.

Going To School: From Five Years On

Just as a nod to the bigger picture, because I previously had no idea and this arrives quicker than you'd expect. Your tiny little baby who only yesterday was wearing nappies will go to primary school in September of the year they turn five, staying until they reach the age of eleven. They then go on to secondary school, where they will learn to grunt and smoke fags.

Note: *None of the above is guaranteed. If you're in any way concerned about any developmental issues, consult your doctor or your health visitor.*

And there endeth the book.
Good luck with everything you encounter
and really, don't worry about a thing.

You will be fine.

Acknowledgements

Thanks to all the mums and dads who gave me their invaluable time and insight for this book. You are all good people. Also, much gratitude to all at Michael O'Mara, particularly Gabriella Nemeth for your tireless work, Louise Dixon for the yes, and Toby Buchan for the insight and expertise.

INDEX